Praise for *How to Say It®* t

"David Solie's *How to Say It to Seniors* is an invaluable tool for any insurance or financial professional working with older consumers. He offers meaningful insights, useful tools, and pragmatic advice not just on how to better communicate with consumers, but how to better help them fulfill their needs and aspirations. Mr. Solie's book should be required reading for anyone engaged in this market."

—Alan Katz, past president of National Association of Health Underwriters

"This is a terrific book! David Solie has beautifully integrated his knowledge of child development into later development. His fresh insights into the psychology of older adults combined with his practical approach to improving communication between the generations are to be applauded."

—Richard Krugman, MD, dean of the University of
Colorado School of Medicine

"Geriatric psychologist Solie does an excellent job of debunking the myth that our elders are merely older versions of ourselves. Seniors are undergoing a developmental transition akin to adolescence; practical, effective communication methods are presented to help minimize generational conflict. This, in turn, paves the way for the important work of advocating for (instead of marginalizing) elders, who face a daily struggle for control. This [book] makes an important contribution to our cultural understanding of *seniors*."

—Douglas C. Lord, *Library Journal*

"It doesn't take too extensive a reading of demographic trends in America to know that David Solie has his finger on the pulse of the future. Unlike other books describing the crisis surrounding the aging issue, which point out myriad problems with no solutions, David actually offers a fundamental practical breakthrough in the most crucial area of all: communication. His breakthrough has the quality of genius about it. When you read it you smack your forehead and say, 'Well, of course. It's so obvious!' Millions of readers will have the same response."

—Dan Sullivan, president of The Strategic Coach, Inc.

continued...

"This isn't theory...it's field reality...and David gives the reader practical how-to tips that should resonate with all of us. This book is a great gift for a financial advisor to give to all clients with senior parents. They'll thank you for the lessons that they are not going to learn anywhere else."
    —Dick Bell, CLU, ChFC, CFP, RHU, REBC, MSFS
    2004 president of the Society of Financial Service Professionals

"David Solie's book is full of information, wisdom, illuminating and memorable anecdotes, and practical advice."
    —James Douglas Pittman, CLU, CFP

"All baby boomers need to read this book."
    —Robert W. Griffith, editor of HealthandAge.com

"Every now and then a new work comes along that once you read it, it forever changes the way you see the world. *How To Say It to Seniors* is one of those rare books."
    —Charles D. Hayes, author of *Beyond the American Dream*

"This book is wonderful in the dignity it offers the aged. It shows that they are often dealing with clusters of losses and could use support, not hurried answers. Readers will learn that the elderly are not being stubborn or meandering just to be difficult—instead, they are tending to the job of being old."
    —*Chicago Tribune*

How to Say It®
to Seniors

CLOSING THE COMMUNICATION
GAP WITH OUR ELDERS

———

David Solie, M.S., P.A.

PRENTICE HALL PRESS

PRENTICE HALL PRESS
Published by the Penguin Group
Penguin Group (USA) Inc.
375 Hudson Street, New York, New York 10014, USA
Penguin Group (Canada), 90 Eglinton Avenue East, Suite 700, Toronto, Ontario M4P 2Y3, Canada
(a division of Pearson Penguin Canada Inc.)
Penguin Books Ltd., 80 Strand, London WC2R 0RL, England
Penguin Group Ireland, 25 St. Stephen's Green, Dublin 2, Ireland (a division of Penguin Books Ltd.)
Penguin Group (Australia), 250 Camberwell Road, Camberwell, Victoria 3124, Australia
(a division of Pearson Australia Group Pty. Ltd.)
Penguin Books India Pvt. Ltd., 11 Community Centre, Panchsheel Park, New Delhi—110 017, India
Penguin Group (NZ), 67 Apollo Drive, Rosedale, North Shore 0632, New Zealand
(a division of Pearson New Zealand Ltd.)
Penguin Books (South Africa) (Pty.) Ltd., 24 Sturdee Avenue, Rosebank, Johannesburg 2196,
South Africa

Penguin Books Ltd., Registered Offices: 80 Strand, London WC2R 0RL, England

While the author had made every effort to provide accurate telephone numbers and Internet addresses at the time of publication, neither the publisher nor the author assumes any responsibility for errors, or for changes that occur after publication. Further, the publisher does not have any control over and does not assume any responsibility for author or third-party websites or their content.

HOW TO SAY IT TO SENIORS

First Prentice Hall Press edition: September 2004

Prentice Hall Press trade paperback ISBN: 978-0-7352-0380-8

PRINTED IN THE UNITED STATES OF AMERICA

30   29   28   27   26   25   24

Most Prentice Hall Press books are available at special quantity discounts for bulk purchases for sales promotions, premiums, fund-raising, or educational use. Special books, or book excerpts, can also be created to fit specific needs. For details, write: Special Markets, Penguin Group (USA) Inc., 375 Hudson Street, New York, New York 10014.

I dedicate this book to my wife, Janet,
and my two daughters, Kristyn and Gretta.
Your love has made all the difference.

Contents

PART THREE

NEW STRATEGIES FOR COMMUNICATING WITH OLDER ADULTS

Foreword

We are all faced with an aging population in our parents, neighbors, friends, colleagues at work, and clients in the office with whom we must effectively interact. How many times have we felt frustration and misunderstandings with this group, who frequently need our help but seem to resist us at every turn? In my twenty years as a physician and teacher specializing in geriatric medicine, I have been in countless situations where communication issues with older persons were the crucial element in their own survival. Why won't they take the medicines I prescribe? Why do they insist on talking about things that seem irrelevant to their situation? Why do they resist changes that would so clearly benefit them?

Get ready for lightbulbs to flash and a feeling of "aha!" when you read in the following pages David Solie's remarkable approach to improving your interactions with the seniors you encounter every day. Mr. Solie has a unique background that informs this book: training and experience as a health professional that preceded an outstanding career in business. His success is due in large part to his remarkable communication abilities, which he has continually developed and enhanced over the years. In this book he shares his insight and research to enable all of us to overcome the challenges of communicating with older adults.

I have spent most of my medical career caring for older persons in a variety of settings and teaching medical students and physician trainees about the field of geriatrics. And, even as I write this foreword, I am caring for an elderly parent who is recovering from an illness. I have found Mr. Solie's insights extremely useful and applicable to both my medical work and my interactions with my own parents. Reading this delightful book was not only enjoyable but triggered a flood of memories of older adults that gave me a new understanding of "why they do the things they do." I'm recommending it to my friends and anyone who comes in contact with this age group, and I know you will benefit from the information it contains in all your dealings with older adults.

Mary Elina Ferris, M.D., M.S.Ed.
Associate Clinical Professor of Family Medicine
University of Southern California School of Medicine

Acknowledgments

This book began as an idea, one that I resisted for a number of years. In the end, the idea overcame my reluctance and evolved into a finished manuscript. But the idea needed more than my efforts to make the journey to a book. It needed the collective talents of others to become a finished product.

First and foremost, the writing of this book has been a partnership between Susan A. Schwartz and myself. Susan has not only been instrumental in translating my ideas into a book, she has been an invaluable partner in developing it into its present form. I am deeply grateful for her friendship, professionalism, insights, and dedication.

The glue of our writing partnership has been my assistant, Ilene Burgard. Ilene not only kept the project on track and moving forward, she experienced firsthand the reality of the book's material with her own parents. I am grateful for her professional skills and inspired by her love and dedication to her parents.

The emotional glue of my writing process has been by wife, Janet. She is a consummate professional whose reading and recommendations came at a critical time in the book's development. As important, she has given me the encouragement and flexibility I needed to write the book.

I would also like to acknowledge my literary agent, Jane Dystel, and her staff at Dystel and Goderich Literary Management for their unwavering support and professionalism, as well as our editors at Prentice Hall Press: John Duff, who saw the potential in the proposal as first presented; and Christel Winkler, who guided this work from proposal to finished book and beyond. I am also grateful for the sharp eye and skillful editing of copyeditor Collette Stockton.

Along the way to the idea for the book were many people whose influence prepared me for the task. Dr. Henry Silver taught me to challenge my assumptions and look for other possibilities. Sister Mary Catherine taught me that insight and compassion are inseparable. Dr. Peter Lesson taught me the art of clinical medicine with older adults. Mildred Swanson taught me that the best things in life are understood with the help of others; similarly, my mother-in-law, Rita O'Shea, showed me firsthand the importance of social connections in the life of senior adults. Dr. Richard Krugman taught me to think without restrictions while keeping a well-tuned sense of humor. Barry Wolfe believed in my talents long before I did. Dan Sullivan taught me the great freedom and joy of finding one's own unique ability.

Although names and identifying details have been changed, I am also grateful to the many patients and clients who have given of themselves and their life stories. In some cases they were unaware that they were casting their legacy into realms of life they never dreamed possible, legacies that would offer comfort to people they would never meet or know. Whether in a nursing-home bed or the conference room of a prestigious financial organization, these individuals shared the drama and "secret stuff" of their hearts. I was honored to be a part of that process and the lessons it provided.

Last, my mother, Carol Solie, has an important role in this book. She proved to be part of the catalyst in my search for better answers to issues regarding how we communicate with older adults. Even in conflict she has taught me invaluable lessons about aging and the needs of older adults. She has lived her life based on the belief that it is not what you say, but what you do that defines who you are.

Introduction

"Age is an opportunity no less than youth itself,
though in another dress."

—H. W. Longfellow

THIS book explores the reasons why communicating with the elderly is sometimes so frustrating and offers strategies and skills for overcoming these difficulties. In these pages, I show that by understanding our senior adults' unique developmental agendas and using different language, phrases, and vocabulary, anyone—relatives, friends, colleagues—can learn to communicate effectively and effortlessly with their aging family members, acquaintances, and clients.

Aimed at baby boomers and their parents, professionals who work with the elderly, and everyone who has regular contact with seniors and finds conversations at times to be an exercise in frustration, this book offers the insights I've formed in serving this segment of the population over the past twenty-five years. The book has four aims:

- to help readers understand the conflicting and previously unappreciated tasks on the senior adult's unique developmental agenda;

- to recognize how these developmental tasks can interfere with our ability to communicate effectively;

- to offer easy-to-learn skills that enhance communication between the generations;

- to guide us in becoming advocates for our elders.

A unique agenda? Developmental tasks? What, we may ask, could possibly be "developing" in the psychological makeup of the elderly? Many of us look at members of our parents' generation and see a diminished version of the vibrant people we once knew. We observe that they move more slowly and aren't as physically strong as they used to be. In conversation they tend to repeat stories they've told us a dozen times or can't seem to stick to one subject. They fret over inconsequential details or abruptly end important conversations before anything has been resolved. They didn't act or talk this way before they got old. So surely they aren't developing anymore, because we can see them declining right before our eyes.

This book explodes the "myth of diminished capacity" in our elders and offers a new way to interpret these behaviors. It also illuminates the enormity of the psychological journey the elderly face and how we can help them understand it. By examining the elderly person's two developmental drivers—**maintaining control** and **searching for a legacy**—and how those drivers conflict with each other and with our own agenda, by looking at how these conflicts manifest themselves in their unique communication habits, and by understanding the predictable dilemmas the elderly face as they age, we develop a sense of how tough it is to be old and how brave our senior citizens are. Our understanding of "strength" deepens as we come to realize the unique strength of the elderly.

The fourth aim of this book, and perhaps the most significant, is to introduce the idea that we need to become advocates for the older generation. One of the primary tasks that engage the elderly is the search for a legacy by which they'll be remembered. Every day, whether our elders speak of it or not, they are reexamining events in their lives with the enhanced perspective of age. It is an all-consuming task, one that does not come naturally to us for two reasons: *first,* because for most of our lives we've been obsessively moving forward, *second,* because of what Mary Pipher, in her book *Another Country,* calls the loss of the communal society that once nurtured this process.

I grew up at the tail end of this communal era, because when I was young my grandmother lived four blocks away, and my aunts, uncles, and cousins also lived within walking distance. My extended family congregated at Grandma's house quite frequently. It was the period in my life when I felt most secure. After my grandmother died, everyone started to move to distant cities, and I now realize that my safety net, with all my family in one place, disappeared.

When our society lost this communal network, many aspects of our culture died, including the fact that we lost contact with older family members who could give us perspective on our lives. Without that perspective, we've become overscheduled, hyperstimulated, and culturally grumpy. We are so burdened by the pace of our lives that when we must interact with older people who cannot keep up, we run out of patience trying to fit them into our schedules. We have forgotten—or never learned—how to value our senior adults' advice. As they begin to slow down, we push them aside so they don't impede our progress. While we may accomplish a lot every day, we don't necessarily feel good about our achievements because no one is there to tell us about the longer-term implications of choices we make. Many of us assume some things about senior adults that aren't true, and then can't understand why we aren't getting along better with this aging population.

Seniors in turn don't benefit from our ability to help them with their end-of-life tasks. They become developmental orphans, and their search for legacy, which must be helped along by caring younger adults, doesn't take place. Why? Because sadly we don't make the time or possess the skills to do it. Once we understand their age-based agenda and how its conflicting demands are expressed, we serve no higher purpose to our elders than to aid them in this search. I call this process *legacy coaching;* it is a demanding job, but also one of the most rewarding tasks we will ever assume.

FOR the last seventeen years, I have served as medical director and CEO of Second Opinion Insurance Services, a brokerage that specializes in the insurance needs of impaired-risk, elderly individuals who are not the usual candidates for life-insurance policies, but who need to get them (usually for estate-planning purposes). My job, which is to obtain life-insurance policies for seniors at reasonable rates, uses my educational background in developmental psychology and my training in medicine.

I've been successful for two reasons: First, I use skills for representing my clients to the life-insurance industry that maximize the optimism about their life expectancy. While I cannot change medical facts, I can provide an intelligent, researched assessment of their condition. Second, I have developed unique communication strategies—the ones presented in this book—for working with older clients. These strategies have afforded me repeated opportunities to review new cases every year where other professionals—estate and financial planners, attorneys, trust officers, and financial advisors—have failed to achieve the desired outcome. Why? Because of repeated episodes of what I call "elder frustration," or the inability to interact effectively with this age group. These well-educated professionals think they are asking the right questions, but their lack of understanding of older adults' developmental agendas prevents them from connecting with their clients' heartfelt concerns. Because of this lack of connection, these clients tend to summarily reject their advice. More often than not, these pros have drawn up elaborate proposals that lay out millions of dollars in savings to their client's heirs, only to have the elderly client dismiss everything in the plan. Similar frustrations arise every day as we deal with our aging parents.

A few years after I established Second Opinion in 1985, my largest account took note of my ability to communicate with and get great outcomes for elderly clients, and asked me to develop guidelines its own top advisors could follow in dealing with elder frustration. This assignment came as I began to resolve difficulties with my mother, then in her mid seventies. Recently widowed, she had locked horns with me when I took charge of settling my father's estate. Communicating with her about these matters, as well as her reluctance to seek medical care she urgently needed, was more of a challenge than I'd bargained for. I had to develop ways to communicate with her that would accomplish what I needed to know and yet not leave her feeling more bereft or scared than she already felt.

Also, at the request of my largest key accounts that include some of America's most well-known financial institutions, I began to lecture regularly to professional groups about the insights I've gleaned from my interviews with the elderly. These are tough groups to speak to; the soft subjects don't usually interest them. But these professionals experience repeated episodes of elder frustration, and want to know how to get beyond it. After hearing this material, they not only understand the special ways they need to start communicating with the elderly but they can put the information into action and get measurable results. Because I know that this information resonates, I know that the material is applicable to nonprofessionals—my fellow baby boomers—as well.

THERE is widespread feeling among my age group that somehow we've failed at trying to communicate with older people, especially our parents. There is a nagging concern that very little of what the generations say to each other sparks real connection. This book shows us why we feel this way and what we can do about it. Nothing in the Aging sections of bookstores and libraries addresses these concerns from an age-based, or developmental, perspective. Most of the available references are what I call the "peppy papers" on how to stay perky despite aging, or the "existential papers" on the grim life of loneliness, uselessness, and boredom that awaits the aged. There are also books on how we can manage the unmanageable older adult. But no book provides a psychological profile that defines what others and I experience in our daily interactions with the elderly. I offer these strategies in an accessible format useful to my fellow baby boomers and colleagues. I believe this is the first book to connect communication difficulties with previously unappreciated developmental conflicts that senior adults must work through as they near the end of their lives.

I approach aging from my personal experience and that of others as it has been related to me. I have developed strategies that make sense from my experience, not from academic studies. One way I present information is to relate compelling stories about situations we all face: How am I going to relate to this elderly person in my life? How can I make our conversations more meaningful? I hope this information provides insight about what's happening in the tugs of war and verbal battles I've had with my family and clients. From these situations, I hope to convey a new way to think about this person and what may be driving difficult behavior, fussiness, attention to detail, or the repetitive nature of conversations. I have attempted to create a scenario, discuss the dynamic, and offer action points that may be useful in similar situations.

Most of the unsettling behavior of older people is the result of developmental tasks operating quite intensely in a world that is hostile to them. If we were still living in a communal society, we would revere our elders and their legacies would emerge in a formal way. Control would not be an issue because they would be supported in dealing with their losses (loss being the reason they are so focused on retaining control). Further, we would have learned the skills needed to facilitate their legacy search. But we've ripped "elders," a term of respect, out of our vocabulary; now they're just "old." And they have to fight to express their age-appropriate desires in a culture that does not understand what their desires are, nor what is truly motivating their behavior.

If we learn how to nourish our elders developmentally, much the way parents learn how to guide the younger generation, then we open up a rich lode of experience from which we can draw, and that older person will be remembered in exactly the way he or she wants to be. This book shows us how we can change the nature of our relationship with our elders—to mine the richness they possess—with just a few words. These words may not always work, but if we don't give up (just as we'd never give up on the younger generation), things start to shift into a different and very rewarding gear.

Communication is a skill. If we ask the right questions, we'll get meaningful answers. In order to ask those questions, we need to use language that connects and allows the person to reveal secrets. Contained in those secrets are the nuggets that suggest legacy. If we minimize or dismiss this process, we lose credibility with that person. We also lose the sense of our own integrity. Knowing that this legacy task exists is half the battle. Facilitating it is what this book addresses.

Where this book begins its pioneering work is in recognizing that, at the end of life, personality development is still taking place and that the elderly feel a developmental conflict similar to those that grip all of us at every stage of life. If we learn to recognize the ways in which our elders express their conflict, we can offer simple and effective strategies to enhance our ability to communicate with them. *How to Say It to Seniors* suggests ways we can enhance our relationships with senior adults in our lives by learning how to:

■ appreciate their age-based agendas;

■ minimize the clash with our own internal agendas;

■ master a few easy communication strategies to facilitate their end-of-life tasks;

■ enhance our ability to offer the kinds of language and nonverbal reinforcements that allow better communication.

This book is meant to be both enlightening and practical. The first part presents my thinking about what causes the exasperating verbal and nonverbal behaviors we observe in our elders. Later sections offer practical skills for bridging communication gaps that result from these difficult behaviors. I encourage you to turn first to those sections or chapters that most directly apply to your situation with your elderly relative, colleague, client, or friend, then return to the more theoretical underpinnings of the advice you read.

The goal of *How to Say It to Seniors* is to help readers improve their relationships with this elderly generation that deserves our best efforts in facilitating their compelling end-of-life tasks. By doing so, we have the privilege of retrieving a world that might be lost to us forever and enriching our lives in ways we can't imagine.

PART ONE

HOLDING ON AND LETTING GO:

The Unappreciated Agendas of Older Adults

———

This section focuses on the unappreciated but profoundly important items that drive the developmental agendas of older adults. Working through these urgent yet conflicting items can produce verbal and nonverbal behavior that baffles those of us who are not as far along in the aging process. Before attempting to understand how our elders express these conflicts, we have to know what those conflicts are—and how they differ from ours at midlife.

ONE

Different Missions, Different Agendas

HOW THE AGING PROCESS AFFECTS COMMUNICATION

---

*"Before you contradict an old man,
my fair friend, you should endeavor to understand him."*

—George Santayana

The Driving Test

I was sitting next to an elderly couple and their fifty-something son early one Sunday morning in a quiet café. From the moment they were seated it was clear the son was irritated with his parents. He tried to hurry their breakfast order, balked at his father's attempt to make small talk with the server, and brushed off his mother's suggestions to let his father "have some fun." His mood made it clear that this family gathering was not about fun. Once they placed their food order, he launched into a discussion of a "family problem" involving his father.

The father, who appeared to be in his eighties, was scheduled to take a written driving test in order to renew his license. The problem, from the son's perspective, was his father's inadequate preparation for the test. The father tried to explain what he was doing to prepare by offering his ideas on test taking in general. He even wanted to discuss how much the "rules of the road" had changed since he was a boy. His son would have no part of that discussion. He hammered home the message that his dad "just didn't get it." He repeatedly interrupted his parents to point out the lameness of the content of their conversation. "Here is what you need to know," the son insisted, "to pass the test."

Sitting there and listening to this exchange I heard two distinct voices. From the son I heard a steady flow of anxiety, scolding, sarcasm, impatience, and lecturing, tinged with frustration and anger. From the parents I heard embarrassment, puzzlement, shame, guilt, and inadequacy, also fraught with frustration and anger. Their collective resentment soon filled the room. Their food got cold. The bill came none too soon.

Most people assume that getting old is just more of the same. Aging is seen as being an adult, just older. This is what the son saw when he looked at his parents: older versions of the people they had always been. Somehow in the aging process they had become less effective at organizing and managing their daily lives. His job was to help them overcome these deficiencies so they could stay on task. He needed to keep them focused and help them get things done. It annoyed him that his parents seemed unaware of how far they had fallen off the pace. What about a simple written test did the old man not understand? Why did preparing for this test have to be so complicated an issue between them?

It was clear to me that the son's questions to his father were not getting him near his goal of facilitating the test taking. So what if the son's assumption—that his father "just didn't get it"—was wrong? What if the aging process demands that older adults undertake a completely different tack in their lives that is totally foreign to anyone who is not yet old? What if the elderly are on a mission that is not only far more complicated than the son appreciates, but would also prove to be the most significant of their lives? If we assume these questions are worth asking, then a clear gap exists between the middle-aged son's assumptions about what's important to his aging father and what his father considers to be important—about test taking as well as life's bigger issues. This gap in the son's knowledge about the real mission of aging is what may have been causing their communication difficulties. If the son wanted to achieve meaningful dialogue and change a chronic pattern of conflict with his parents, he would need to know more about their mission, and how it differs from his middle-age concerns.

The Geriatric Gap:
The Secret Mission of Older Adults

On any day in any major city in this country, we can find dozens of courses on child development, but not a single course on geriatric development. In fact, the term "geriatric development" strikes many of us as an oxymoron, a contradiction in terms. What kind of "development" could possibly be taking place in elderly people, whom we observe to be in a state of general decline: slowing down, losing their faculties, turning inward, and becoming increasingly set in their ways and stuck in the past? Why do we have nearly infinite patience for a two-year-old's communication challenges—sometimes in the form of a tantrum—and almost no patience with a seventy-nine-year-old widow when she quietly changes her mind about a well-conceived plan to revise her financial statements, or our elderly relatives when they start repeating a story we've heard many times? Are we being ageist? Are we engaging in a double standard—patient with our difficult children, impatient with "difficult" older adults? If the answer is yes, is something else at work? Do we lack key information about the aging process and how it affects our elders? If we had such information, would it help us appreciate what they're going through and enhance our ability to communicate with them?

To answer these questions, we need to address what I call a "geriatric gap" in our understanding of the way personality develops throughout our lives, and specifically how this lack of knowledge affects our interactions with senior adults. After World War II, when a lot of children were born, parents became more child focused than their parents had been. In the postwar, baby-boom years, there was a need for these parents to understand their children and how they developed. The goal was to become better at nurturing this younger generation. Our parents took our developmental mission to heart. They bought millions of copies of *Dr. Spock's Baby and Child Care*. Beyond Dr. Spock, theories of personality development set forth by Piaget and Erikson,

among others, once the province of academics, were popularized and consumed by this child-focused generation. Certain terms emerged as part of the
vernacular. Our parents may have referred to the "terrible twos" and understood the reasons for temper tantrums. "Identity crisis," a popular term to describe the conflicts of adolescence, is one we may have used to describe
ourselves when we started to mature.

This cultural understanding of childhood was not always so. Back when
"children should be seen and not heard" was the generally accepted parenting
model, there was less patience for childhood's unique developmental agendas,
in part because earning a living during the Depression, when our parents were
young, was so difficult. But when more children showed up in the baby-boom
years after WWII, that model was gradually replaced by a more child-friendly
understanding of the underlying psychological conflicts every child works
through on his or her way to maturity. The stages of development we see in
children were proposed, tested, and retested, and found to be helpful tools in
raising healthy, well-adjusted kids.

While personality development models in children have been well described, we are still in the Dark Ages about how such models apply to
middle-aged and older adults. We use some terms to describe aging beyond
the early adult years; for example, the meanings of "midlife crisis" and
"empty-nest syndrome" are generally understood in our culture. But we
have no such terms or models to apply to the elderly. In fact, we wonder if
such models exist for this age group, because what common experiences
could older adults be dealing with? They've all led such different lives and
strike us as a varied bunch. We think we know how to be successful in raising children, and we have a pretty good idea of what motivates our middle-
age personalities, but we've never been old ourselves and don't know what
that experience feels like. We have difficulties communicating with older
adults, but each person seems to have different issues that are expressed in
various ways.

Is there a set of common issues that motivate senior adults? If so, what are
these issues and can we learn to appreciate them? If we appreciate them, would
we be better able to communicate with and nurture our parents and others of
their generation as they age? What are the developmental tasks associated with

getting old and how can knowledge of them enhance our ability to communicate with this age group?

Personality Development: Growth through "Crisis"

To answer these questions, we need to understand the basics of personality development—how we acquire the tools needed to manage the journey from infancy to adulthood and into old age. If we understand this process, we can appreciate what motivates the elderly, and why we sometimes clash with them. Our newfound knowledge can help us close the geriatric gap in our understanding of older adults because we can begin to realize that the behavior we see as "diminished" in elderly parents, clients, and friends actually exists to do a very specific developmental job.

A word of caution: Describing anyone from a developmental perspective is interesting and useful, but this is only one aspect of personality—a tool that may help us improve our ability to communicate. Those who regularly interact with elderly parents or clients will find this information useful in understanding why the elderly tend to act and react as they do.

In each stage of life, so the theory of personality development goes, an individual must deal with a pair of tasks that conflict. This conflict motivates our behavior, even though we aren't aware of it. Erik Erikson, a towering figure in the field of psychoanalysis and human development, referred to these conflicting tasks as "crises" that we must resolve in order to move *forward* to the next stage of our development. If we don't resolve the key issues at each stage, we may get stuck and be considered immature by our peers.

In the case of the elderly, their attempts to resolve their developmental "crisis" propel them *backward,* not forward, to reflect on what their lives have meant—to themselves, their loved ones, and the world at large. When we observe the ways senior adults sometimes communicate—by repeating stories, or fretting about details, or forgetting things—we may think that they're becoming frail or losing their grip. Nothing is further from the truth. In fact, this communication style may indicate that seniors are responding to their developmental tasks (also called drivers or motivators) in a compelling and urgent way.

Why the urgency? If they are able to respond to their developmental mandate and resolve their conflict, they will be remembered for their time here on earth and cherished by succeeding generations. If not, they fear their lives will fade away and be forgotten.

The Two-Year-Old's Crisis

Let's look at the developmental crisis of a two-year-old, who needs Mom but also needs to begin the long process of separating from her and developing an independent identity. These two needs are contradictory and produce a conflict that the child finds difficult to resolve. Note that children don't choose to deal with these conflicting needs; they are not even aware of them. Sometimes, while trying to resolve the tricky conflict—needing Mom and needing to be separate from Mom—children balk or throw a tantrum, which is a perfect expression of the difficulty of resolving the conflict. Only by having a tantrum (which expresses the need for independence) and also having mom there (to offer comfort and manage the crisis) can the child resolve it and toddle off to the next developmental stage, which has its own set of conflicts that drive the child's behavior.

How do parents respond to two-year-olds having tantrums? We manage this task as best we can—giving them space, love, guidance, and understanding. One thing we learn *not* to do is to punish children for this behavior, because experts tell us that doing so could actually delay achievement of the independence children are struggling to attain.

The Teenager's Crisis

Teenagers have similar developmental drivers: needing independence from parents ("Get out of my face!") while preserving parental protection ("May I borrow twenty dollars?"). Though more verbal than two-year-olds, teens find resolving the conflict between their developmental drivers just as difficult and do so with equally disruptive behavior. Instead of throwing tantrums, however, they might totally withdraw from their parents, or lecture them, or engage in risky behavior that causes us to doubt their sanity.

How do parents help teenagers resolve their developmental crisis? Much the same way we respond to two-year-olds, giving them patience, guidance, and space to take the risks that allow them to learn and mature from those experiences.

The Adult's Crisis

What are the developmental tasks of adulthood? In early adulthood, we experience a crisis between our newly found independence and a need to develop intimacy with others, or a significant other. Ironically, just as we achieve our lifelong dream to be independent, we begin to look for a partner with whom we will give up some of that independence. Many young adults use the aforementioned term "identity crisis" to describe the conflict they feel, but most of us work through this crisis, come to terms with our independence and our urge to merge, and move into the next developmental stage, that of middle adulthood.

In middle adulthood, having resolved the conflict between achieving independence and giving some of it up, we begin to feel we're at the peak of our game. Because we have acquired all the confidence-building experience we think we need, we feel powerful, independent, and in control of our lives. Yet at this stage, we are also pulled in different directions: still raising children and—because people are living longer than they did in previous generations—sometimes taking care of elderly parents. Just as we arrive at our performance peak, ready to go all out for our careers or other personal interests, we begin to feel the conflicting need to give something back to other generations. Erikson calls middle adulthood the time of life when we are "generational"; that is, we want to express our strengths solely for personal gain, yet also feel a conflicting need to use our power to nurture others and contribute to society.

How do we resolve this conflict? Some of us never do. Artists, the proverbial mad scientists, and workaholics of every stripe focus their energies and creativity exclusively on themselves and ignore the conflicting driver that tells them to nurture other generations. But most of us in this middle-adult stage realize that despite our ability to soar to new heights, we must also be rooted in society. Therefore we focus some of our energy in ways that contribute to something beyond ourselves: raising our children, volunteering for community organizations, and the like. If we do not address this conflict—find balance in our lives—we fear we'll arrive at the end of life alone, with our energies spent, and be unable to cope with the demands of a long and difficult old age.

The resolution of early adulthood's developmental drivers is usually a marriage, a surrender of two independent lives to create one solid union. The resolution of the middle adulthood drivers—the conflict between ego gratification and civic duty—is an investment in the future, a marriage to something bigger than ourselves. Yet, these two developmental pushes of adulthood have one thing in common: a sense of control over our lives and destinies that we take for granted. Sure, some things will happen we can't control: fate intervenes or we have a run of bad luck. The person we want to marry marries someone else. A couple of career breaks don't go our way. But we are confident of our abilities and generally get to select where we want to go: We marry someone else, embark on another career path, decide when to become parents, and choose what civic duties will engage us.

Imagine our discomfort when we begin to realize that these powerful feelings don't last. Although we haven't personally experienced old age, we observe that our elders no longer seem focused on the future; they want to dwell primarily on the past. This powerful feeling of middle adulthood has waned in them, and we conclude it might not exist in later years. We see that older people are no longer at the top of their game—don't even seem concerned about it—so we assume they are in decline.

But could something else be replacing these feelings of peak power in the psyches of our elders? If so, what is driving the developmental agendas of people at this stage of life?

The "Secret Mission" of Older Adults

What we as a culture have failed to recognize in the theories about personality development is, simply, that it is a lifelong event: These crises continue well into old age. We have become quite good at understanding the personality drivers of children and younger adults; however, we often fail to appreciate what happens when we get old. Why? We've all been two years old, and most of us have raised children who are traveling through various stages on the road to adulthood. But no middle-aged person knows how it feels to be seventy. Without firsthand experience, how can we effectively nurture the elderly? We can't possibly provide them with support for their end-of-life tasks if we don't know what those tasks are.

As a culture, we've been suckered into thinking that the deterioration we see in senior adults is the common experience of this age group. So what could possibly be driving them forward developmentally? We look at older adults, interact with them regularly, do our best to communicate with them, and all we sense from them is a desire to reflect backward, not forward, in their thinking. We notice they can sometimes be as tempermental as two-year-olds or teenagers, with behavior that can be just as irritating. What is going on that makes them so difficult?

If personality development is a lifelong process, then at the end of life, the elderly face a developmental conflict they have trouble expressing but must resolve. Seniors' developmental tasks compel them to **maintain control** over their lives in the face of almost daily losses, and simultaneously to **discover their legacy,** or that which will live on after them. I describe this conflict as needing to hang on tight while also needing to let go and discover the meaning of their lives. These tasks are so important, and have such an impact on our daily interactions with older adults, that we examine them in detail in the next two chapters.

Trying to resolve this conflict sometimes produces a "difficult" communication style. The elderly will wander from subject to subject, repeat stories we've heard dozens of times, postpone decisions, go off on tangents, or describe something in endless detail. We look in depth at these unique communication styles—and how to respond to them—in chapter 5.

Such verbal behavior can be frustrating to us, because we haven't learned to appreciate the tasks on their agendas. After all, we're at the top of our game. We need to load up the fax machine, whip out that Palm Pilot, make endless lists, and cross off as many items as possible every single day. That process makes the middle-aged feel powerful and in control, as indeed we are. When we encounter these older adults, who move at a snail's pace, we get frustrated and blame them for their supposed infirmities.

That frustration is the crux of our difficulties with senior adults. I call it the clash of two different age-based agendas. We need to slay those dragons and achieve as much as we can, but elderly people have very different motivators. Control, as we'll discuss in the next chapter, is slipping from their grasp daily, as their health fails and their peer group fades away. Control isn't an issue for the middle-aged—we have it, we know it, and we use it—but for a seventy-year-old in failing health, it's a huge issue, because when it begins to slip away, many elderly people feel the need to hang on to everything they can. Rather than see old people as diminished, we need to understand that their drivers do a different job: resolve the conflict between the need for control and the need for reflection in order to discover their legacy.

This conflict between hanging on and letting go produces a communication style that we see as diminished or difficult, but the way our elders communicate contains clues to the urgency they feel in trying to resolve these items on their agendas. Only by understanding these behaviors can we begin to improve our relationships with this generation and help them complete their compelling end-of-life tasks.

Facilitating the Crisis

Now that we understand the dynamics of aging in a totally different way, let's again consider the breakfast meeting that opened this chapter. The son, with his middle-age developmental agenda, was feeling powerful and in control. His experience behind the wheel and in renewing his driver license several times helped him focus the discussion with his father about how to approach the exam. Yet he wasn't connecting with the older man's concerns. Why? Because his parents were responding to their own developmental drivers that were steering them in a different direction. They wanted to approach the matter *their* way, with the test itself taking a backseat to their memories of what driving has meant to them throughout the years. The result: a complete communication breakdown.

How different would the discussion have been had their son realized that passing the written test was not the issue for these eighty-something parents. What was important to them was remaining in control of the process, pass or fail. Had the son known about these developmental tasks, he might have responded in the following way.

How to Say It:

"Tell me, Dad, how have *the 'rules of the road' changed since you first got your license?"*

I guarantee he would have had a more meaningful and productive conversation with his father if he had.

As we'll see in later chapters, in almost every conversation with an older adult, control and legacy issues rise to the surface. By listening for and responding to those verbal cues, we can bridge this geriatric gap and facilitate their end-of-life tasks. Once we understand this gap and begin to appreciate it, the clash fades away. How? Because we stop fighting our elders for the one thing they will not surrender: the control they need to manage their lives and shape their legacies.

TWO

The Need for Control

"You cannot shake hands with a clenched fist."

—Indira Gandhi

The House

One of my best friends recently went through a tough time with his eighty-three-year-old widowed mom that illustrates the difficulties many of us experience in dealing with our aging parents. This lovely woman would not leave the family home, a charming but run-down Queen Anne structure tucked into a steep Seattle hillside. The woman's mind was as sharp and her spirit as lively as the day she graduated from high school, but she'd had one hip replaced, the other hip was causing her quite a bit of pain, and she found it difficult to climb stairs. The house she refused to leave had no bedroom or bathroom on the main floor; the kitchen was a "firetrap," according to my friend; the roof leaked and needed to be replaced; the exterior needed a complete new paint job; and the yard was overgrown and unsightly. My friend and his sister tried everything to get their mother to move into an assisted-living facility, but she refused. Money was not the issue: Their father had left her with $3 million in CDs sitting in a Seattle bank. When reason failed to budge her, they threatened her, and then they tried guilt: "You know, one day we'll come here and find you on the floor, unable to get up. You might even die that way." Her response: "Where would you like me to be when you find me? Under the kitchen table? On the stairs? Out in the garden? Where?"

The two forty-something siblings became so distraught they eventually sought counseling. The counselor's advice: Stop fighting your mother. Fighting hasn't worked. Facilitate her instead.

So my friend and his sister went back to their mom and said, "Okay, Mom. You want to stay here? Here's what we're going to do. We need to install a bathroom on the first floor so you don't have to climb stairs. We'll make an appointment with the fire inspector so that when we remodel the kitchen, we do it in accordance with modern fire code. The roof leaks and will have to be replaced. We'll hire workers to paint the outside of the house. As for the garden, we'll call someone to . . ."

Her response: "NO! This old house isn't worth it!" And within three months she had moved, with a woman from her church, into a beautifully appointed assisted-living facility just outside the city.

DOES this situation sound familiar? If it doesn't, it will. Either you or someone you know will one day be faced with the task of persuading elderly parents, relatives, clients, or acquaintances to move from the treasured family homestead. I know dozens of baby boomers who have told me essentially the same story as the one above. The question is, what happened to make this Seattle mom change her mind after years of stonewalling her children? This chapter explores the developmental need of elderly people to "hang on tight," how that need can create communication difficulties, and the consequences of not allowing the elderly to maintain the control they feel they must have.

To **maintain control** is a primary driver for the elderly, because each day, they feel losses—of strength, health, peers, and authority—that are staggering. As the losses mount, real control over their lives, their health, their living arrangements, even their sense of who they are, is slowly slipping from their grasp. The constant feeling that they are losing control is manifest in various ways, not the least of which is the sometimes negative manner in which they express themselves. Once we understand how profoundly the control driver is operating beneath the surface, motivating almost every move they make, we will be able to appreciate and facilitate our elders in their end-of-life tasks. Once we learn the importance of assisting and not fighting them, communication will become more pleasurable, productive, and effective.

The Magnitude of Loss for the Elderly

What, we may wonder, is bringing this compelling developmental need for control to the surface in older people? The overwhelming feeling of loss that accompanies old age creates their need to "hang on tight" to whatever they possibly can. Loss isn't something that motivates younger generations, because our developmental drivers are compelling us constantly to move forward. We do experience loss—loss of a relationship, a job, a parent, or elderly colleague—but we possess the physical and psychic energy to replace those losses with something else—a new partner, a new work arrangement, a new lifestyle. We're aware of our power and sense of control that enables us to move on.

The elderly, however, find it a lot more difficult to cope with loss. In some areas, the losses simply cannot be regained or replaced. Some of the losses the elderly experience are more obvious to us than others.

Loss of physical strength: We know that as we age we lose strength, but before we become old, there always seems to be a quick fix available in the form of different pep pills, better nutrition and exercise, more sleep, longer vacations. No one under the age of seventy can appreciate what it's like to lose strength and not be able to get it back. The intensity with which the elderly experience the body's loss of strength has a profound impact on their sense of who they are.

Imagine what it would be like if *you* developed the flu and were asked, when you're sacked out in bed with sweats, aches, and a fever so high you can't lift your head off the pillow, to make an important decision, such as where you'll live for the next twenty years! Many elderly people comment that making such important decisions is difficult because they don't have the strength to cope with the details. The task seems overwhelming, much as it would be to us if we were fighting a temporary fever. Yet older people may be battling the losses imposed by the chronic condition of old age and we want them to move? How could we demand that of our elders when we ourselves could not make that kind of life-altering decision under such circumstances?

Loss of health: It's not unusual for the seventy-plus age group to make more visits to the doctor, take more medications, and get sick more often than those of us in middle age, but when they visit the doctor, they're not presenting the sore throats and colds or strained muscles from which we seek relief. Our elders may be dealing with life-threatening conditions that must be treated, followed, and medicated on a daily basis. Just as they reach the stage of life where they have fewer responsibilities and the time to enjoy themselves, their bodies begin to betray them in ways that they simply can't control.

Loss of peer group: Once health begins to slip, people in their seventies begin to lose friends and members of their social groups at an alarming rate. In Germany, deaths are announced via black-bordered cards sent in the mail. An eighty-year-old woman I know there, a friend of my mother's, receives two or three of these cards every month. She reaches into her mailbox, pulls out a black-bordered card, and there's no mistaking that her peer group has just lost another member. Imagine what it would be like to lose even one friend with whom you've shared your life's stories for decades?

Those are some of the obvious losses our elders face, but there are other areas of loss that aren't as obvious, yet are just as deeply felt.

Loss of consultative authority: Ours is not a culture that values the wisdom of our elders. There is little chance for us to come together and use the wisdom accumulated through their years of living as a resource that enriches our lives. We seem to want to segregate them into communities of other older people, so that their perspective is not available to us. We tend to see older folks as diminished, high-maintenance versions of ourselves.

In the corporate world, consultants advise CEOs to hire and reward the high potentials, usually bright, young, but relatively inexperienced workers who are nurtured and developed for the fresh ideas they may bring to an organization. While this trend may be waning, for decades older workers, with their vast knowledge of a company's history, have not been valued, and have been eased out to make room for younger workers.

On the home front, Granny usually doesn't live with the family anymore (whose members are rarely at home anyway, thanks to the scheduling demands of a two-career family). Because of the pace of our modern lives, we rarely have time to sit down and enjoy a leisurely chat that invites the older person to share wisdom about family matters. While loss of consultative authority is not necessarily a given in other cultures, it is a huge factor in ours, and our elders feel it. This particular loss hammers seniors with the message that they no longer have a social purpose. While loss of health or strength are of concern, this loss signals to them that they don't count in the culture and can lead them to feel isolated and depressed. It's not just that we don't go to Grandma for advice; we send her a message that she has no advice worthy of our consideration.

Loss of identity: One person I would not want to be around for twelve months after he retires is Mr. Corporate Executive. Mr. Important, used to ordering FedEx, calling a meeting, and getting on a jet at a moment's notice, suddenly can't get his phone calls returned. He may visit his old place of employment, but his former coworkers treat his presence as a social event, and after some pleasant chitchat, dismiss him, roll up their sleeves, and get back to work. Loss of identity was painfully rendered in the movie *About Schmidt,* in the scene where Schmidt, recently retired and at loose ends, puts on a suit one day and goes back to the office to have a chat with his successor. Remember how the younger executive responded to Schmidt's attempt to impart wisdom about the job he'd just assumed? The actor didn't actually do this, but he conveyed an image of rolling his eyes and counting the seconds before Schmidt left, so he could get on with the important tasks that filled his day. Schmidt picks up on this younger colleague's impatience to get back to work, leaves the building, then notices all his files—a lifetime of his professional activities—discarded and waiting to be carted away. Although Schmidt didn't admit to his wife what happened at the office, that visit reinforced his awareness of his loss of identity.

Women who worked as homemakers all their lives also feel a loss of identity, usually at a somewhat later age, when their husbands die and they are no longer part of a marital team. Many women who survive their spouses find themselves exposed, no longer a part of the comingled identity they shared when they were married. Even women who were not particularly happily married become quite anxious at the thought of widowhood. I know one senior who moved to another part of the country because she could not adjust to being single among the social group that knew her as a married woman.

Loss of physical space: Face it: We really don't want to worry about the elderly. We want them to go someplace—assisted living or a retirement village—where they'll be safe and well cared for and part of a community of old folks just like themselves. The house or condo that was once their sanctuary, as we saw in this chapter's opening vignette, has become a safety hazard, threatening the older person's very existence. But a person's identity may be closely tied to the comforts of the physical space he or she has occupied for years. Even more important than the comfort the space provides is its role as a repository for memories seniors must sort through in the search for the way they want to be remembered. The elderly seem to be less concerned about the safety and convenience provided by something unfamiliar than they are about the risks involved in preserving the familiar. They are not focusing on safety; they are dealing with issues much larger and more important to them than convenience.

Loss of financial independence: Many seniors fear being poor, particularly widows or widowers who depended on their spouses' incomes to meet financial obligations. Combine that with the high cost of living and the fact that everyone is living such a long time, and they begin to fear they might run out of money. The financial freedom they took for granted during their high-earning years may elude them in old age when all else is failing, too. Actually, "freedom" when it comes to finances is too strong a word, for this senior group has always been very frugal. They clearly remember the financial hardships their families experienced during the Great Depression, and how they had to scrimp and save to raise us and put us through college. They refuse to understand that the price of a long-distance phone call has dropped to a small percentage of their children's monthly income. The only thing scarier to them than running out of money is becoming financially dependent on the younger generation, which thinks nothing about spending two and a half dollars for a cup of designer coffee.

Or consider this: You work all your life to build up that nest egg and some thirty-year-old high-potential financial advisor comes up with a plan to save your heirs a bundle in inheritance taxes. The lawyers say that if you redraft this document and transfer that amount to somewhere over *there,* it'll make a lot more sense. But does such a transfer really make more sense to the older person who is already dealing with substantial losses and thought these

financial matters were settled ages ago? The plans may make sense to our focused, middle-aged, "slay-the-dragons" mentality, but all the elderly person
can do is say NO!

NO!

Where have we heard this word, loudly, clearly, and forcefully before? Remember our encounters with toddlers whose developmental drivers compel
them to pull away from, but also to cling close to Mom? Or adolescents, who
need to form their identity separate from the family, but aren't yet ready to
break away completely? How is that conflict expressed? Sometimes by simply
saying NO!

The elderly feel a similar need to say NO! that comes from deep within,
because when everything around them seems to be giving way, sometimes the
only control they can exercise is to say NO! Anything *we* say or do that erodes
what little they still control can be met with almost irrational resistance. It
seems as though they would rather be in control than be logical or socially appropriate. What compels them to say NO! so often?

Maintaining control is a need in the elderly almost as necessary as breathing and certainly as compelling as a toddler's need to say NO!, which is the
perfect expression of the confusion he's feeling about wanting Mom but also
wanting independence from her. He's *confused, but compelled* to try to resolve the disconnect.

In a similar way, the elderly feel compelled to maintain control as they
face daily losses. While a certain amount of control is important to all of us,
we now appreciate that the elderly live in a world where they feel they are
losing everything—their strength, their health, their peer group, even their
identity—basic stuff that makes them who they are. And now we want to
propose to them that they change their living space or their wills? NO! is
sometimes the only appropriate response they can make to the conflicts they
are feeling not only internally but also with us. Remember that the drivers
imposed by our own developmental agenda compel *us* to get things done,
make decisions, and act on them. Our drivers can clash with theirs that compel them to hang on tight and to reflect.

Dealing with NO!

How do we typically deal with an elderly person's NO? We mutter under our breath, secretly doubting their sanity or worrying about the onset of dementia. We punish them in some way for what we perceive to be their stubbornness. We are quick to show them the error of their ways. We jump on them, second-guess them, and try to strip them of what little control they have. No wonder we get stonewalled, as the siblings in the opening vignette did. No wonder we experience an uncomfortable interruption of communication. No wonder we can't connect. Do we punish them intentionally? Of course not! We simply fail to respond to the dynamic driving their behavior.

A friend of mine, Roger, told me a tale similar to the one that opens this chapter. His parents are still living in the suburban New York home in which he grew up. The home is not being properly maintained and his father is getting so frail he can no longer climb the stairs to the second-floor bathroom or install storm windows stored in the basement. Roger, whose job requires a fair amount of travel, spent a year trying to convince his parents to move, but they refused. Their argument: We're very private people. Moving to assisted living feels to us like living in a fishbowl. Besides, we don't want to see a lot of old people who depend on canes and walkers (even though Roger's mother now uses a cane to keep her balance). After a year of discussion that got him nowhere, Roger tried one more tactic: He brought his reluctant parents to his therapist, who was about the same age as his parents. "My fear," Roger confided, "is that my parents will think he's 'very nice' but they won't get anything out of the session." And that's exactly what happened.

But after the session, something changed for Roger. He backed off, gave up the fight, and resigned himself to support the life his parents want to continue to lead. He realizes his role as their facilitator is a time-consuming and energy-draining responsibility he doesn't relish, but one that will enable them to live as independently as possible for as long as they wish. He'll have to remodel the house to accommodate their infirmities and hire workers to do basic upkeep, but he concluded that's a small price to pay for a more peaceful relationship with them, one that allows them to put the control issue to rest.

"After the session, I realized the part my two siblings and I were playing in this impasse. My parents told my therapist that 'the children' still had lots of stuff in the house, even though we moved out decades ago. I realized that some of the problem for my parents was that their declining physical strength rendered them unable to deal with our stored possessions. So now, every time I visit them, I make a point to either throw stuff out or take it back to my apartment. But I've backed off from questioning their decision to remain in the house. It wasn't getting us anywhere."

Sometimes the best way to deal with this particular control issue is to *back off*. But what, we ask, if the difficulty is something potentially life-threatening: their health? Though health issues seem to be a different matter, they really aren't. We may think getting elderly parents to take medication on time, or seeing doctors when they should, is an entirely different category. And we may be correct, up to a point. But we can't forget that the control driver is always operating, even when a person is close to death, as it was with my eighty-six-year-old grandmother, who was suffering from congestive heart failure.

A dramatic example of the loss of control—and how *not* to deal with it—is what happened to her. At the end of her life, she found herself in a hospital room being treated for her heart condition. She realized that she did not want to die in the hospital, so in the middle of the night she got out of bed, packed her bags, and called her oldest daughter to pick her up and take her home. When the night nurse found my grandmother dressed and ready to leave the hospital, she alerted the on-call physician, who ordered my grandmother back to her hospital bed and physically restrained.

The next morning this physician came by to visit. Grandmother demanded that he remove the restraints, which he agreed to do, but lectured her on the need to cooperate with his instructions. As he stood at the end of her bed referring to her chart, she reached over to a bowl of fruit on her nightstand, picked up an orange, and tossed it at him. "Don't ever tie me up again!" she told him as he stood there in shock after the fruit bounced off his forehead. He never got the chance. With the help of her daughter, my grandmother checked herself out of the hospital, went home to her own bed, and died the next night.

If you have any doubt about how important *control* is to an elderly person, remember this story about my grandmother.

The Redemptive Power of Backing Off

An amazing thing happens when we back off and stop badgering senior adults to do something they are resisting for whatever reason: We give them room to resolve the conflict. Look at the elderly woman from Seattle. The moment her children backed off from their demands to move out of the house, she decided to move. What was the dynamic at work? At last, her children handed her the baton that placed control of this major decision where it belongs—with her. They stopped demanding that she move, told her of plans to facilitate her wishes, and gave her some space to consider what was involved in renovating a dilapidated house. The language they had been using for years was working against the driver that compelled her to hang on to the familiar. Once they stopped using this pressuring language and she heard that control was back on her side, she felt free to make a different decision.

If you encounter resistance from an elderly parent, client, or customer, try rephrasing your concern into a statement or question that offers control.

How to Say It:

Fifty-something woman to elderly parent: *"Mom, I sense you don't like the idea of selling the house. I won't mention the subject again, but I'd like to hear your ideas about how we'll maintain it!"*

Nurse to elderly patient: *"Mrs. Jones, I realize you prefer to see Dr. Philips, but since he's running late, may I help you with any questions about those new dosages?"*

Sales clerk to senior customer: *"I'm sorry we don't have that style in stock. Do you want to choose another style or shall I call you when your first choice comes in?"*

We look at other examples of specific language useful in addressing control issues in chapters 5 and 9.

The Problem with Not *Backing Off*

What happens when we don't recognize the control issue for what it is? The fight for control is as compelling to the elderly as the need we have to check items off our daily to-do lists. Take away control and the person will fight to get it back; in fact, they will become so focused on that particular issue that the other equally compelling developmental issue—searching for a legacy, or how they'll be remembered—may never get addressed.

If there isn't some intervention or advocacy on behalf of seniors, then this control issue, left to its own volition, will overwhelm them and force them to spend most of their time trying to manage it.

The fight for control can undermine and sabotage the resolution of a person's developmental crisis. Imagine what would happen if you punished a two-year-old for having a tantrum! What you get is a child so focused on avoiding punishment that he or she never learns to make independent choices. The result of the inability to make independent choices is the fostering of dependent, fearful, dysfunctional, angry children. Without the ability to play out the dynamic, what results in a child—or an elderly person—is a great distortion of that dynamic and no resolution of the developmental crisis. Remember that this distortion goes on beneath the surface. It's rarely verbalized directly. In a child, it profoundly affects personality development. With most senior adults, lack of control over their lives causes them to be consumed by this single issue and they never get to focus on an even larger issue, the legacy issue, which is discussed in the next chapter.

Why do we fight our elders for control? It's partly the result of our own developmental drivers pushing us to get things done, and partly because we might have serious and legitimate concerns about their health and safety.

There's a nursing home in Montreal that takes this control issue quite seriously, and many such facilities are following their lead. As we'll discuss more fully in chapter 4, this facility posts thirty-one "rights" of their elderly residents that are inviolable: the right to privacy, the right to control their living space (meaning that everyone from medical doctors to custodians must knock before entering their rooms), the right to be informed about anything that affects them personally, the right to dignity and respect, even the right to refuse medical advice once the risks are explained. One woman resident grew so frail she was having difficulty moving around, even with her walker. The medical staff felt the time had come for her to be confined to a wheelchair, and so advised her, but she refused. After being apprised of the risks of falling if she continued to use the walker, and what a fall at her age would do to her, she was allowed to make the decision she felt was the right one for her, one that preserved her dignity and freedom of movement.

We tend to justify wresting control from our elders because it's "for their own good," but we're usually urging them to do something for *our* own good. We treat them as though they are incapable of making any choice at a time when control is a burning issue with them. What we must do instead is step back, hand them the control baton, and allow them to run with it.

How to Say It:

Lawyer to senior client: "You're right, Mr. Jones. In my eagerness to clinch this deal, I may have rushed you about signing these documents. Do you need more time to consider selling this property?"

Losing a Legacy

What happens to toddlers denied developmental breathing room? Though it may be years before it's expressed, these children will not be able to resolve this conflict over the need for independence and the need for maternal protection. They can become so focused on avoiding punishment that they fail to express the very real need they have for independence. What can result are children incapable of taking risks, who remains stuck in a dependency that isn't healthy or advisable. Maturity is delayed or never achieved and what results are individuals who grow up to be fearful, conservative, and generally unhappy.

What happens to senior adults who are not allowed to exert control over their lives is even more profound than squelching a child's need for independence. As we learned in the last chapter, these developmental tasks occur in pairs and they are not optional. They are driving a person whether the person is able to express them or not. If the control issue is not resolved, then seniors adults will continue to fight for it. This battle will go on and on, with its resulting communication failures, until their last breath. Sadly, if they are continually fighting the battle for control, these seniors will never get to the equally compelling driver on the old-age agenda—the search for a legacy. As we discuss in the next chapter, the discovery of legacy is a profound experience, not only for the old person, but for anyone who comes in contact with that person. But until the need for control is met, there will be little or no effort expended on the reflective process needed for this awesome task.

Up until old age, our developmental drivers pushed us forward—relentlessly—to the next hurdle on the road to maturity. But in old age, the driver pushing us forward is actually bringing us to a retrospective phase that commands us to review our lives. For senior adults to go forward developmentally, they must first go back and take stock of what has happened. But if control battles continue until death, seniors don't have the chance to reflect and formulate their legacy—those events and values by which they want to be remembered by family, friends, and future generations. Without resolution of these final developmental drivers, that legacy will be murky at best and, tragically, may never emerge at all. It's the difference between a life that fades away and one that is cherished by succeeding generations. That's why it's extremely important to recognize an older person's need for control and facilitate it every way we can.

THREE

Legacy: The Need to Be Remembered

"And none will hear the postman's knock without a quickening of the heart. For who can bear to feel himself forgotten?"

—W. H. Auden, "Night Mail"

The Perfect Plan

I was once called into a case involving a seventy-eight-year-old mogul who had built an engineering empire that was valued at more than $40 million. His financial advisors developed an elaborate plan to save his heirs about $20 million in estate taxes. On presentation day, the mogul walked into the meeting with his wife and their thirty-something son, who sported a turtleneck sweater and a ponytail. The advisors carefully laid out their plan, complete with pie charts, graphs, and tables presented in gorgeous four-color PowerPoint slides, and then waited for the mogul's reaction. "Now, let me see if I understand this plan," he began. "If we do nothing, then he"—referring to but not naming his son—"gets twenty million dollars, and if we follow your plan, he gets forty million dollars. Correct?"

"Yes!" exclaimed the advisors, practically in unison. "Yes, it's clear that you understand what this plan is trying to achieve."

"Well," replied the mogul, "that's about thirty-nine million, nine hundred thousand dollars more than he's worth." And in one gesture, he swept all the materials off the table and exited the conference room, with his wife and Mr. Ponytail trailing behind and not having said one word.

You can imagine the shock of the financial professionals seated at that conference table. How could this mogul, who is obviously so brilliant, not see the wisdom and the beauty of their plan? How could he reject the advice of the very men he hired to advise him? Even more puzzling, why wouldn't he want to his son to benefit from a perfectly legal way to preserve his hard-earned wealth?

Every day, whether they are millionaire moguls or retired postal clerks, former CEOs or homemakers par excellence, our elders are engaged in an elaborate process of reviewing their lives to find something of meaning that will last long after they depart. Some get the urge to write their life stories in elaborate detail, or make an oral history using a tape recorder. But whether they express it or not, life review is the dominant psychological event of getting old. The need to be remembered, to uncover their lasting legacy, is the other urgent developmental task confronting the elderly. Once they feel that control is no longer an issue, senior adults focus on reviewing their lives to find what it meant for them to have lived.

CONFLICTING with the need to exert control, the need to create a legacy ferments beneath the surface of our seniors' awareness. While they feel a subconscious urge to hang on tight, they are also faced with the daunting task of discovering how they'll be remembered. How do these two needs conflict? If seniors feel they do not have enough control over daily events, they spend all their time fighting for it. That fight leaves them no physical or psychic energy to relax into the reflective mode needed to review past events, the preliminary step necessary to form their legacy. Fulfilling this aspect of their developmental mandate is the opposite of maintaining control: It is the ultimate process of letting go.

Through this life review process, a person's legacy may emerge in several different forms, but only one is heartfelt and meaningful. How successful the elderly are in discovering any aspect of their legacy depends on how successful *we* are in helping them through the process.

This role of legacy coach, mentioned in the introduction and discussed more fully in chapter 6, is one we must take as seriously as we did the job of parenting. One of our greatest roles as parents is to provide a safe environment for children to pass from one developmental stage to the next. The formidable challenge of legacy coaches is to provide seniors the same kind of safety net that gives them the support they need to explore their past. Undeniably challenging, the role of legacy coach also offers us the greatest rewards.

The Task of Being Remembered

Why is this process of life review so significant? Why do our elders need guidance from us? In developmental terms, the conflicting drivers we've experienced from childhood up to but not including old age have propelled us *forward* to the next developmental stage. Each succeeding stage presents itself as a kind of change of attitude or direction.

- For the two-year-old, dependence on Mom now becomes a goal to become independent.

- For the teen, dependence on parents morphs into the goal of moving out of the house and living independently.

- For the young adult, self-reliance transforms into the goal of surrendering some of that newfound independence by forming a family.

- For the midlife adult, achieving family life and career satisfaction compels us to make a contribution to the world around us.

The resolution of the conflict between each of these pairs of conflicting drivers propels us forward to the next stage of development.

But if we're fortunate to live long enough, we reach a stage where our strength ebbs, losses accumulate, and the main event we face is the end of life. Most of the people who have known us for decades are no longer around: Either they've moved, or we have, or they are no longer living. It's at this stage that we pause to reflect, to look *backward,* perhaps for the first time, and try to assess what our lives have meant—to us and the world. Because no previous developmental stages were reflective ones, most people don't have the skills to tackle this job. In order to prepare it, we must resolve our need for control with our need to let our energy, thoughts, and emotions *go* to have the strength and clarity necessary for what we are compelled to do.

Control we understand on a gut level. As middle-aged adults, we don't spend much time or energy thinking about it. We have it and exercise it every day. But this other developmental task—searching for our legacy—is not something we so readily understand. A thorough life review prior to old age is what we do only when we suffer a devastating loss—of a parent, job, friendship, or relationship that meant a lot to us. At those times, we may look back and remember the event and the role it played in our lives. But that review process doesn't last very long, because our developmental drivers are propelling us forward. We take a deep breath, perhaps learn from the experience that life is too short or unfair, and then move on to the challenges that still lie ahead.

For seniors, though, this look backward is a vital part of their conscious and subconscious existence. Every day, every hour, whether they mention it or not, the seventy-plus age group is reviewing their lives. The review intensifies when health becomes compromised, what Mary Pipher refers to in *Another Country* as moving from the young-old to the old-old stages of life.

Imagine having to make life-changing decisions while coping with chronic pain or fatigue. Most of us would simply put those decisions off until we felt better. Old age can feel very much like having a condition from which the person will never fully recover. There are good days and bad days, but decisions have to be made regardless, because the life-review process is relentless. The elderly begin to sense they don't have the luxury of setting this task aside because they may never feel better than they do right now.

Most people, if they think about it at all, assume this life-review process is an end in itself, serving no real purpose other than to help seniors pass the time. But based on the work I've done with the elderly for the past quarter century, I understand life review as a tool to accomplish a job very different from any we faced as young or middle-aged adults. It is a continuous and involuntary retrospective in which senior adults weigh everything they have done in order to build understanding and acceptance of the life they lived. Suddenly they are called upon to shape out of the mists of their life experience a legacy that is not just politically correct, but also heartfelt and meaningful.

Winding Up Empty

When we start to realize that we're not going to be here forever, we become aware that it's not clear what it meant to be here at all. That awareness is the developmental task looking for airtime and triggering our desire to deal with our legacy. Discovering legacy implies two things: (1) We've arrived at some understanding of our life, and (2) we want to pass along what we've learned. Although we may not know the shape of the legacy we're going to lay down, we're clear about the desire to do so.

When understood as a developmental need, legacy insists on being addressed, either consciously or unconsciously. Yet because seniors are old doesn't mean they understand this process. When faced with it, most people do not have a clue about how to accomplish it and need to be facilitated. A lucky few are focused and have it all figured out. They have clarity about their life and its purpose. The rest of us wind up fuzzy since we don't know where to begin.

THE mogul we met at the start of this chapter was certainly a man in control—he decided to hire these advisors, then indicated the plan they devised did not meet his expectations. What were those expectations? We can assume he'd thought about them, but at the time of this meeting, those thoughts hadn't yet been shaped into a legacy he could articulate. When presented with Mr. Ponytail as a logical choice, he knew what he did *not* want, but he didn't have a vision of what he did want.

Even the most focused, brilliant, and motivated of us can use some help in resolving this conflict between the need for control and the need to let go. The life-review process is difficult for people like this mogul who have been obsessively moving forward and now see that this way of relating to the world has created a barrier preventing them from analyzing some of their actions and decisions. When they look back behind this barrier, they view a landscape that isn't necessarily pretty. Some things have occurred they're not thrilled about. While it's possible that the mogul had a spat with Mr. Ponytail right before this meeting, it's more likely, given his abrupt departure, that he was beginning to understand a deeply felt but long-denied anger about his role, or lack thereof, in his son's life. All of a sudden, when the anesthesia of "doing"—for themselves, their families, or their companies—wears off, seniors such as this mogul have to rethink everything.

AFTER the mogul bolted this meeting, I urged one of the financial planners who knew him well to go back to the family and get more information. "He's searching for his legacy," I commented. "He doesn't know what it is yet. You assumed it was Mr. Ponytail, but Mr. Ponytail doesn't work for him on any level."

Listening for Legacy

In life review, not all past experiences are deemed important. Those that make the cut may be put into a different category or context.

I remember a conversation I had with a seventy-something widow about an insurance policy she was advised to purchase. I was taking her medical history and asked a standard question about the deaths of her parents. She paused before answering, usually a clue that life review is in process. Then rather than giving a brief, fact-filled answer, she told me a story: Her mother died very young by breathing noxious fumes from mixing two cleaning agents in a small windowless bathroom. Her father, upon hearing the news of his wife's death, began to suffer chest pains and was taken to a hospital. Advised to remain overnight for treatment and observation, he refused, went home, and died in his sleep that night of massive heart failure, leaving my client and her sister orphaned before they were ten years old. "I haven't thought about this in years," she told me. "For a long time my extended family and I were very angry with Dad for leaving the hospital when he needed treatment, but *now* I think I understand why he did. He loved my mother so much that he simply couldn't bear the thought of living without her."

Notice that I could have cut her off and written down *Mother: accident; Father: heart attack*. But the way she paused before answering this routine question made me realize that she was forming something more important than a routine response. Rather than rush the moment, I gave her all the time she needed. Her statement about her father indicated that she was reviewing her life and had placed that life-altering event into an entirely different category, one that evoked not anger, but compassion and understanding.

Rabbi Zalman Schachter-Shalomi calls this process *recontextualization,* and it goes with the territory of life review. In his book *From Age-ing to Sage-ing,* Rabbi Schachter-Shalomi describes recontextualization as the process by which senior adults look backward to prepare for their future, remembering long-ago events, people, places, and relationships, and assigning new meaning or importance of these events to their lives. This mandate to look backward for answers to prepare for the future is a process ripe for facilitation and understanding. Here are a few statements or questions that can spark the recontextualization that can lead to legacy.

How to Say It:

Son to elderly father: *"Tell me about the winters you experienced growing up in Wisconsin."*

Young CEO to chairman emeritus: *"How did you recognize that the company was ready to leap to the next level?"*

Health-care aide to elderly patient: *"What made the 'good ole days' so great?"*

Baby boomer to elderly aunt: *"Why are you thinking about your prom date now?"*

Simple communication techniques to facilitate legacy formation are discussed in chapter 10.

The Mandate of Life Review

There is a certain irony connected with all developmental stages. Look at the young adult: As soon as he's out of the house and free from the significant relationship with his parents, he's compelled to surrender much of that autonomy to form his own family. The irony of revealing a legacy is that in order to go forward to accept our lives and prepare for a peaceful death, we must look backward and recontextualize the events we've lived. If we go forward without looking back, the journey is extremely unsatisfactory. Note the way the mogul felt the need to remove himself from the discussion for which he was ill-prepared. He could not articulate his discomfort, but his actions spoke volumes.

Life review isn't about the need to erect a monument in our honor. It is about reviewing what happened in our life and assigning new or different meanings to events, then considering how those recontextualized events figure into the way we want to be remembered. This is a *huge* undertaking, one that most elderly people may not be able to manage on their own.

Once a person enters the life-review zone, the review becomes the mandate. It is relentless. Because it is both a conscious and an unconscious process, life review cannot be set aside. It's always operating—a natural evolution of where a person is going developmentally—whether the person is aware of it or not. The goal in facilitating an older person in the search for legacy is always to bring as much of that process to the surface as possible, so that forming a legacy becomes an articulated, conscientious, and satisfying endeavor.

Not All Legacies Are Created Equal

We all live unique lives. Some are more colorful or complex than others. So it should come as no surprise that we all have the potential to have a unique legacy. The operative word here is "potential" because, sadly, most people die without much assistance in this process. One of the painful realities of American culture is that aging adults are essentially developmental orphans who must fend for themselves without benefit of a nurturing environment. Amy Dickinson was interviewed on the day she officially assumed the role once held by Ann Landers as the *Chicago Tribune*'s syndicated advice columnist. Although she'd already received hundreds of e-mails, Dickinson commented that her first piece of snail mail had arrived. Its author was a seventy-eight-year-old woman who said she felt "invisible." In our fast-paced culture seniors can quickly become derailed, defeated, and overwhelmed. The unfortunate casualty of our twenty-first-century lifestyle is their legacy.

In my estate-planning work with seniors these past decades, I've noted that legacy falls into three main categories: default, political, and organic. Let's look at how each form emerges.

The Default Legacy

A default legacy is a legacy of natural consequences, one that the person has no part in shaping. For whatever reason—usually because the person dies unexpectedly or his final years were consumed with control battles exacerbated by family, friends, or professionals—the person never communicates the way in which he or she wants to be remembered. Therefore, that person's legacy gets shaped by others, possibly the very people with whom he or she was constantly struggling. I don't mean to imply that the default legacy is necessarily a bad one. The children or grandchildren may be part of that legacy, and they in fact may be wonderful people who carry on the person's memory in beautiful, generous, and loving ways. But because no one facilitated the life-review process to discover what was unique about that particular life, the matriarch or patriarch had little or no input into the shape of that legacy.

Another way in which a legacy emerges by default is when survivors are cleaning out the deceased's personal effects and find letters, photographs, diaries, or notes that reveal secrets that the survivors never knew. Sometimes it is formed when the will is read, or a close friend of the deceased shares a story at the memorial service that surprises the family. Sometimes these revelations become part of the deceased's ethos or mystery, and leave the person's legacy in a limited and generally undeveloped form, not useful to the survivors.

Most people want to avoid being remembered by default. It's a passive process and may be a highly inaccurate portrait of their lives.

The Political Legacy

The political legacy can be described as "doing the right thing," more mechanical than heartfelt, more process driven than authentic. Political legacies are formed by people who have completed a limited form of life review and have come up with obvious ways in which they want to be remembered. A doctor leaves enough money for his grandchildren to attend medical school, or donates money to the medical school itself for scholarships for future doctors. A grandmother discusses in detail the food she's cooked for her family, then leaves her recipe box and kitchenware to her grandson, who is studying to be a chef. A mother leaves her son the family automobile and her daughter the household effects. These are examples of political legacies, what one might expect a person to do. These gifts may be heartfelt, or may not be.

If a person is one of those whose legacy is clear—that is, the person has led a focused life and knows exactly how he or she wants to be remembered— then the political legacy may be the heartfelt one as well. The person may not have needed to do a thorough life review, because the life lived was open, un-ambiguous, and full of meaningful deeds. But in many cases, the political legacy may reflect only part of the person's life story.

Consider the mogul, whose advisors thought about his $40 million estate, reviewed changing tax laws, and came up with a way to save his family $20 million in estate taxes, clearly the right thing to do *if* he was interested in a po-litically correct legacy. But he would have none of it. Why? One explanation might be that the politically correct legacy fell short of his estimation of his life's value and how he wanted to be remembered. The meeting reinforced his subconscious sense that he had more legacy work to do. Because he could not say what he wanted, he chose to exercise control by ending the meeting abruptly and making it clear that his advisors would need an entirely different approach to bring him back to the conference table.

The Organic Legacy

An organic legacy comes from the heart and is based on an extensive life re-view that considers every person, action, and event, every road taken or not, and assigns a weight or meaning to it in light of the person's entire lifetime of events, actions, decisions, judgments, and reactions. It is prompted by a con-scious and unconscious awareness, at age seventy and beyond, that one's re-maining time is limited. The organic legacy starts to emerge as a primary developmental mission, not an epiphany. It is predicated on gathering appro-priate data—memories, thoughts, facts, emotions. It is a time-consuming, exhaustive, yet ultimately redemptive process that recontextualizes everything that may have been misinterpreted, misunderstood, or unrepaired in a person's life. How well we facilitate this stage of a person's development has a direct impact on how complete the person's life review will ultimately be, how the person will be remembered, and how well that person's life will impact future generations. Most important, a well-facilitated life-review process affects how peacefully a person faces death.

In the case of the mogul, leaving all his money to his heirs didn't work for him on any level. I credit one of his advisors, who took a risk in his relationship with this man to discover the organic legacy. He got a clue from a conversation he had with the man's wife, who told him a little-known fact about her husband: The mogul had attended college in the Depression, and at the start of more than a few semesters, didn't have enough money to pay his tuition. The college forgave him his debts and, soon consumed by the empire-building phase of his life, the young entrepreneur didn't look back. The advisor played a hunch: He arranged a meeting with the college's current president and called his client. "I know we missed the mark last week and I'm sorry," the advisor told the mogul. "Please give me just fifteen minutes more of your time. I have another idea."

I wasn't at this meeting but was told that the mogul walked into the conference room ready for battle and his entire demeanor changed when he was introduced to his alma mater's current head. Guess how long it took him to decide that the school was to become part of his legacy? Once the president expressed the need to create a tuition fund for the school's incoming and matriculated engineering students, the mogul made his decision to provide these scholarships in less than five minutes. But he had some conditions, among them, his gift was to remain anonymous. The college president agreed, then invited him to tour the campus some weeks later. When the tour was over, the mogul had refined his contribution: Not only would he endow scholarship awards, but the school of engineering was to have a new, updated, and expanded wing named after him. Out there somewhere is a future engineering student, now only four years old, but who will one day want to go to that school, won't have enough tuition, and that mogul's life will be remembered in *exactly* the way he wanted. This is a true organic legacy, meaningful to the person *and* beneficial to future generations.

Organic legacy isn't always a plaque on a wall or a name on an auditorium. It can be many different things: acts of courage, decisions to repair a torn relationship, expressions of loyalty and faith. The process that gets us to organic legacy produces an uneasiness about answers to questions that touch on basic issues in our lives: Have I been a good parent, son, or daughter? A fair boss? A faithful friend? This developmental task triggers life review and then moves it to a much higher purpose: the need to be remembered for the things we valued most.

How do we begin to form an organic legacy, one that is true and heartfelt arising from the mists of a life well lived? How do we get to core issues of our own or another person's life? In the chapters that follow, we'll learn facilitation techniques that can persuade a person to gather outstanding scenes and refine those moments that have defined a life: decisions made and now reconsidered; the person we didn't marry and the one we eventually did; whether we had children, the number we bore, and how we guided them; the career decisions we made and regretted or celebrated. We'll learn not only how to ask the right questions but also how to respond to the answers we hear, answers that hold clues to the values a person cherishes and expresses in almost every conversation. We'll learn how to help seniors shape a lifetime of experiences into the values they find meaningful and with which they wish to be associated.

PART TWO

THE EVERYDAY WORLD OF OLDER ADULTS:

How It Looks, How It Feels, How It Sounds

———

This section explores what older people experience every day as they try—consciously and subconsciously—to resolve the conflicting items on their developmental agendas. The erratic behavior we observe seems to signal that senior adults are "losing it" or "getting on." As this section unfolds, though, we see that such behavior is *not* a sign that the person is declining, but rather reflects a need to transition from the external world to an internal one. Doing so demands the elderly revisit moments in their lives that provided exceptional value to their sense of who they are and how they want to be remembered. This section shows us why it's important to help them in this process.

FOUR

The Myth of Diminished Capacity

"Fear makes the wolf bigger than he is."

—German Proverb

THE prevailing myth about aging—that it is nothing but slow and steady decline—is a by-product of our culture that worships youth and abhors getting old. It is not surprising that this view sees aging as nothing but systems failure when it looks at its older citizens. Bodies don't work as well when we age, so it seems reasonable to assume that brains don't work as well, either. But if this were true, then how do we explain the composition of *Otello* by Verdi, the founding of the *Christian Science Monitor* by Mary Baker Eddy, or the design and construction of New York City's Guggenheim Museum by Frank Lloyd Wright. All of these masterpieces were created by adults between the ages of seventy and ninety-one! A culture obsessed with staying young has missed the most important part of getting old: The brain's physiology changes in ways that promote the person's need for reflection, insight, and innovation.

We know that aging does have its share of medical problems that can have serious mental health repercussions. Mini-strokes, Alzheimer's disease, and depression are only a few examples of how medical problems can create true "diminished capacity" in the elderly population. While the occurrence of these medical problems increases the older a person gets, it is erroneous to assume that all changes in behavior and communication style in this age group are the result of these or other diseases. Our love of the biological model of aging has duped us into believing that "slowing down" is synonymous with diminished capacity. It is one of the most misunderstood and destructive ideas we harbor about aging.

What? we may wonder. Diminished capacity in the elder years a myth? Nonsense! Just look at my seventy-five-year-old mother/colleague/neighbor. She has difficulty getting in and out of the car and now she's repeating herself. Twenty years ago she didn't do that. Must be diminished capacity!

Wrong! What looks like diminished capacity in the majority of the aging population is nothing more than an awareness by that person that he or she is on a different developmental mission. Yes, body parts are breaking down and wearing out, causing the elderly to move more slowly through their days. But research shows that the most important mental capabilities remain intact throughout the aging process. Furthermore, brain functions that do change in old age actually enhance an elderly person's ability to refocus life's priorities from the goal-oriented productivity of our middle-age years to the more re-flective demands of this stage of life.

This myth of diminished capacity has led us to become obsessed with what our elders once could do and now no longer can. Thus we see them as "slowing down," "becoming infirm," "getting difficult," and the like, which causes us to dismiss them on a couple of levels:

- first, as a less productive segment of our society, a society that values productivity above all else;

- second, as a consumer of more and more of society's economic re-sources to stay alive, healthy, and independent.

With these prevailing assumptions at work, the attitude "all is decline" about the elder years can become a self-fulfilling prophecy.

Biology to the Rescue?

In his book (based on the PBS series of the same name) *The Secret Life of the Brain,* Richard Restak, M.D., points to research by Denise Park at the University of Michigan, Ann Arbor, and Marilyn Albert at the Harvard Medical School that indicates that the aging brain does change, but in ways that enhance the tasks we need to do at the end of our lives. According to Dr. Restak, the brain of an older person does show some changes in the prefrontal cortex, its prime platform for working memory capacity and the area responsible for processing new information. But all other brain activities, including IQ and the capacity for verbal expression, language, and abstract thinking, remain gloriously intact. Yes, the body does wear out and slow down—that's a reality of aging. And because of these changes in the prefrontal cortex, the aging brain loses some of its ability to perform multiple mental manipulations. As a result, the external world may begin to fade, distraction set in, and focus becomes compromised. But the slowing of these mental processes *enhances* the ability to reflect and make informed judgments. As Dr. Restak reports, quoting Dr. Park, slowing mental capacity has its advantages.

> While it is true that you get slower with aging, the slowing can actually work to your advantage. For one thing, older people are better at mulling over situations, reflecting, and drawing upon their life experiences to arrive at decisions. (p. 162)

This process Restak describes sounds custom-made for life review and the work of discovering legacy that the older person's developmental agenda demands. Because these changes in the frontal cortex do not affect mental capabilities, the capacity to think doesn't change. Therefore, when we note a "slowing down" or "change" in an elderly person's communication habits, we must look to something other than diminished capacity as a reason. In chapter 5 we'll examine these communication habits—and what they signal—in detail.

While it's true the elderly take longer to process multiple points of information, this lag time allows wisdom to surface that informs every discussion and decision. The body's aging process forces us to stop the frenetic pace of our youth and middle age, and begin to search for the pattern of what's happened in our lives. In doing so, we naturally turn from the external world, with its pagers and cell phones and instant messaging, and focus on our internal world to begin a lengthy life review.

Feeling the Heat

I was once assigned by a large law firm to interview one of their clients who was in the process of preparing her estate. To complete her planning, her irrevocable trust needed to purchase a life-insurance policy. The goal was to insure that a significant portion of her estate, valued at more than $50 million, would pass on to a charity. The question was how long, in my opinion, would she live and how much would she have to pay in premiums on this policy: the longer we could reasonably estimate she was going to live, the lower the premiums.

Because the woman had a complicated health history—I was told the current state of her health was "fair"—I flew to her city to take her medical history in person. I arrived on a midsummer day and began our meeting by casually commenting on the weather.

"Well," she replied, "it may seem warm here, but it's not as hot as where I grew up. I grew up in St. Louis and it was *really* hot there. Except my brother, who couldn't stand the heat and always wanted to leave, married a woman from Atlanta, of all places! So where does he move? To Atlanta! And he's in Atlanta for ten years and he says, 'You know I can't stand the heat, so why am I living here. . . .' "

I thought she understood the purpose of my visit, but where were we? Pretty soon I'd heard all about the divorce and the second wife from Philadelphia, where the weather was much more to the brother's liking, and many more details about her life, which on the surface seemed irrelevant to the task at hand.

What could I conclude from this monologue? Was this woman in the midst of some event that might signal the beginning of further mental or physical decline? Or was something else going on that I needed to understand and respond to? She didn't sequence with me and my midlife agenda, felt no urgency about completing the task before us, because she was responding to a more fundamental need: to revisit events in her life and find new meaning in them. To those of us who aren't clued in, this process can sound like confusion, that they're "slowing down," "wandering off," or "fading before our eyes," when in fact elderly people who engage in this communication style are trying to get a different job done.

This woman from St. Louis was responding to a developmental need—to review her life—that was more urgent to her than my need to review her medical condition. Someone observing her who did not understand this process would certainly conclude she was showing signs of the "diminished capacity" that our culture assumes goes hand in hand with aging. But as Dr. Restak states, aging in the brain of an elderly person would not account for this particular exchange. She was expressive, intelligently responsive, and able to communicate effectively. Clearly there were other factors at work.

Transition Assistance

Recent research on the aging brain makes it clear the changes that occur in older people facilitate this life-review process. What appears to be biological deterioration is the body's way of helping a person transition from the frenetic activity of middle age to reflection in our elder years. What sounds like mental deterioration—fuzzy thinking, repeating family stories, or going into exhaustive detail—actually has a purpose. Rather than deterioration, these communication patterns are tools to assist the transition from "doing" and into the "reflecting" that is necessary for life review, because if senior adults don't get to reflection, they cannot resolve the conflicts of their developmental agendas and come to grips with their lives.

Our elders must get to the point where reflection is their primary focus, their way of understanding their essence. Once they understand their "being," then they've gotten that much closer to forming their legacy and fulfilling their developmental agendas. Physiological deterioration comes to the aid of senior adults because it produces the tools that slow them down to the point where reflection is a lot easier to do.

Lack of urgency is a classic example, demonstrated by the woman from St. Louis and further illustrated in the next chapter. She sensed in me a person who understood her conflict and felt she could take time to reflect on what was uppermost in her mind that day. I assume my reference to the hot weather triggered memories of her brother she needed to sort through as she faced the task of the estate planning that might lead to her legacy. Lack of urgency is a prerequisite for reflection, because otherwise we would have no reason to stop "doing." Why this incessant need to "do"? It's a habit difficult to break because our culture tells us we have almost no value unless we are productive. Older adults need an assist to slow down, and that assist often comes from the biology of our later years.

Look at any previous developmental stage, for example the toddler, who feels the need to separate from Mom. The communication tool of choice is a tantrum. With the tantrum the child forcefully signals he's ready to move to the next developmental stage. As parents we're happy to give him the support to do so.

The elderly also develop communication tools that signal they are ready to fulfill the demands of their new agenda, which is to do the kind of reflection on life's experiences that leads to the discovery of their legacy. Those of us who haven't reached this stage may label these tools as "diminished," but to the elderly, they are anything but.

Rather than pathology, the communication patterns of older adults signal a struggle with significant issues they may not understand. Their communication habits are neither random nor the result of diminished capacity. Instead these habits exist to allow them to resolve this developmental conflict and move toward an acceptance of their lives.

Not every older adult willingly accepts the mandate to slow down and engage in life review. As we observed in last chapter's engineering mogul, the life-review process is difficult for people who have been obsessively moving forward and now have to look backward. They begin to realize, in part because their brain's frontal cortex physiology is changing in ways to aid the process, that their constant forward motion has not allowed them to analyze some of their actions and decisions, and when they look back, they don't always like what they see. One is reminded of the scene in *About Schmidt* where Schmidt is sitting on top of his enormous RV late at night, talking to distant stars and addressing his deceased wife, imploring her to forgive him for being a less-than-perfect husband. It's clear he's just started to realize what impact he had on the two women who greeted him every night for decades. That's where our role as nurturers can shorten the process the elderly undergo to discover what's meaningful to them. If Schmidt had had such nurturing, he might have uncovered this dark side of his legacy earlier and spared himself the pain of his daughter's not-so-subtle rejection.

The myth of diminished capacity assumes that the elderly person's biology and psychology are parallel elements in the older person's life—and they are *not*. As the body slows or fails, the person's psychological mission changes. We need to learn how to nurture this process from "doing" to "reflecting." Typically we've managed it by medicating and segregating the individual. Without proper nurturing, the most profound part of a person's life may get smothered.

Our society manages the process of biological deterioration economically and efficiently: We gather the elderly in assisted-living facilities or nursing homes, depending on the degree of deterioration, and care for them there. We justify these actions by convincing ourselves (rarely the older person) that placement in such facilities is "for their own good"; they'll be with peers and receive the medical care and treatment they need. The trouble with this solution is that often it doesn't address the psychological needs of the older person. These current models address the physical, biological, and medical needs of the elderly, but we know in our hearts there is more to older folks than these elder-care residences address. We know there's more we could learn from our elders if we were more consistently connected to their emotional lives.

Avoiding Developmental Orphans

Harry Harlow and other experimental psychologists proposed the hierarchy of human needs. As part of their research, they separated infant monkeys from their mothers at birth and raised them in two different environments not unlike orphanages or nursing homes: several baby monkeys to a room, their hunger, thirst, and medical needs met. One group was deprived of all human touching, cuddling, talking, and interaction. The other group was cuddled, stimulated, and played with, in addition to its basic needs being met. It isn't hard to guess which group of monkeys thrived and which didn't.

Orphan children deprived of psychological stimulation and touching never learn to interact with other people. They never become socialized. They are emotionally isolated. They are not properly nurtured. They become depressed and withdrawn. Does this scenario sound familiar?

Similarly, older adults in assisted-living facilities or nursing homes in many cases are missing two vital elements that make life worth living. *First,* they miss a consistent connection with a caring adult, someone who has an inkling of what the elder years are like, or the time and patience to listen as the elderly person tries to explain it. Our elders may have time to reflect on their lives and discover their legacy, but without the facilitation of a caring adult— someone who has a stake in the process, someone who may even be a beneficiary of that person's life review—many elderly people who don't engage in the world are lost. They are in the existential crisis of abandonment. They are lonely and become withdrawn and disconnected. The common feeling they have is one of the orphan, disconnected from life with no nurturing.

Second, they miss something even more basic to human happiness, what I would call the normal hum and flow of life created when different age groups interact. There is a variety of experience that comes with that package. I remember taking one of my uncles out of a nursing home for a day trip with one of my cousins. The nurse cautioned us before we left that Uncle Tommy was on a restricted diet. A few hours later, we asked him if he wanted to stop for a bite to eat. "Yes!" he exclaimed, "Let's go get some *real food!*" So off we drove to a local burger joint. When his bacon cheeseburger arrived, along with fries and a beer, his face lit up with a smile we hadn't seen in years. All of us were smiling as we strained to hear each other talk over the loud voices and raucous background music. We lingered over this meal because it was clear to us that Uncle Tommy was enjoying this slice of life without restrictions. He wasn't ready to return to his sterile world. He wanted to feel engaged again and not think about the consequences of his dietary splurge.

That afternoon with my uncle had a big impact on me and helped form my belief that we need to learn the facilitation techniques of legacy coaching and practice them regularly with our elderly acquaintances. These techniques require nothing more than our time and attention and a willingness to engage with the older person. At first the notion that we are nurturing older adults might seem foreign to us. But as we become more attuned and legacy begins to unfold, we see the person not as diminished but as a fountain of information destined to become part of our own legacies in the future.

How can we pass this opportunity by? The minute we reach the age where we begin to say, "Is this all there is to life?" we realize there must be more going on within our elders than we previously thought. We start to reconsider these "diminished" elderly people as essential, not peripheral, to the fabric of our lives.

A woman I'll call Carol, who attended one of my seminars on communicating with elderly clients, came up to me afterward and told me of an incident with her mom, with whom she'd never had a particularly close relationship. The eighty-nine-year-old woman went into a coma and, after a few weeks, doctors advised Carol to pull the plug. For reasons she could not explain, Carol did not take the doctors' advice. Something in her gut told her there was more life left in her mother. After three months of noncommunication, her mother woke up one morning, asked what day it was and then demanded to speak with her daughter, who lived thousands of miles away. The reason for this urgency? She wanted to know if Carol had remembered to pay her (the mother's) property taxes.

Carol told me that in the few remaining months of her mother's life, they shared more than they had in their entire lifetime together. Admittedly an extreme example, but was Carol's elderly mother "diminished"? Physically, perhaps. Mentally? Hardly.

I don't mean to imply that assisted-living environments and nursing homes don't have a role in our society. Sometimes they are the best option we have. We understand they aren't a perfect solution. But we need to consider that the way they're typically managed is a prototype of the way they could be run and there's room for improvement. In addition to emphasis on physical care, more attention needs to be paid to emotional well-being.

Résidence Yvon-Brunet

There's a nursing home—a public institution—in Montreal called Résidence Yvon-Brunet that puts as much emphasis on "home" as it does on "nursing." I mentioned Yvon-Brunet in chapter 2, but it is relevant to this discussion of the myth of diminished capacity. Residents there, no matter what their physical capabilities, are given a bill of thirty-one rights based on respect for the freedom of each person. Yvon-Brunet views old age as a stage of life, not a disease. The facility views itself not as an institution, but as the person's home. Just as you would knock on the door before entering a person's dwelling, everyone from medical directors to janitors must knock on residents' doors and be granted permission to enter. Residents may also lock that door, if they so desire, a basic right forbidden in many institutional settings.

A primary goal of Résidence Yvon-Brunet is to maintain the elderly person's interest in life. In the basement is a complete "Main Street" with shops that look like those of the 1910s and 1920s, when most of the residents were young. Residents look forward to getting their hair done at the beauty shop, shopping at the five-and-dime, going to the picture show, etc. Some other of the residents' thirty-one rights: to know the names of all staff members and what departments they work for; to be told the consequences of any medical procedure suggested—and to refuse the procedure if so desired. The elderly residents at Résidence Yvon-Brunet are free to express opinions, criticisms, and suggestions regarding life in the home. Residents have the right to organize their living space any way they wish.

What makes the rights so valuable is that control issues rarely arise to overwhelm the residents. Although they may have some physical limitations, they have no restrictions on the life of their minds and emotions. The facility recognizes that when biology restricts mobility, the person's psychological state becomes the key to maintaining good general health. At Yvon-Brunet, ambulatory status is unimportant; it's the residents' psychological health that the facility is interested in.

Many baby boomers with whom I've discussed Résidence Yvon-Brunet have an immediate response: It sounds like a better model for elder care than the one we've developed here. It balances the need for special assistance with the need to remain engaged with life. It causes us to rethink our role in seniors' lives. Seeing our elderly as diminished, nonproductive, high-maintenance people is fundamentally wrong. Becoming their legacy coaches suddenly seems more than a good idea; it is our mandate toward rehabilitating older folks into the fabric of life.

Building Our Own Legacies

There's another reason for our renewed interest in the well-being of seniors: We're not that far away from the time when we'll begin to search for our own legacies. Why not accumulate the skills to help ourselves as well as others, as we discover what there is to our histories that might become part of our future. Not to take the opportunity to engage our elders would make us that much less skilled going forward. If we don't learn something about the aging process now, in twenty years our own happiness could be compromised.

Part of the myth we buy into about the aging process is that biology is destiny and determines everything the older person can do, feel, and think. We assume that outside of biological issues, there isn't much else to say about this age group. But once we become clued in to an elderly person's developmental agenda, we realize they are less concerned with biology than they are with maintaining the control they need to fulfill their mission. That mission is *not* to come to terms with their impending death, but to make sense of their life.

This is a different view of aging, one that doesn't accept the notion that slowing down, confusing speech patterns, and physical frailty are "diminished" at all. In my view, what we sometimes see as changes as a part of the aging process are assisting, not hindering, the tasks elderly people must perform to fulfill the conflicting demands of their developmental agendas, which are to be in control when they're losing all control and to let go enough to uncover the legacy that will live on after them. The slowing down that we note, the constant attention to detail, another recitation of a story we've heard many times, or an inability to stick to one subject are communication tools that facilitate the need to review their lives. It is through this life-review process that, given the proper encouragement, they uncover their legacy. As their facilitators, we reap the rewards of that process by developing skills that enhance our enjoyment of the person, enrich and clarify our lives, and encourage the formation of our own legacy.

FIVE

The Communication Habits
of the Elderly

WHAT DO THEY LOOK LIKE? HOW DO THEY SOUND?
WHAT DO THEY REVEAL?

Let the wise listen and add to their learning
and let the discerning get guidance.

—*Proverbs 1:5*

WE'VE now had a glimpse into the conflicts produced by the developmental tasks of our elderly friends, relatives, and colleagues. These tasks demand that the elderly **maintain control** of everything they possibly can, yet at the same time open up and **discover the legacy** that will live on after them. They sometimes express this conflict with behavior—verbal and otherwise—that can strike us as baffling at best, deeply concerning at worst. We may wonder why they sometimes repeat stories we've heard many times before, or seem incapable of answering the same question we ask, and wander from subject to subject, or offer more detail than we want. Their communication patterns make us wonder about their mental acuity or whether something is going on that might require medical attention.

In this chapter we look at these communication habits from a different perspective—as an expression of the conflict the elderly are experiencing in resolving the items on their developmental agenda. As we read real-life examples drawn from my personal and professional experiences, we recognize verbal patterns we've often heard in our loved ones or colleagues. What these patterns reveal may surprise us. In later chapters, we'll explore in more detail how to respond to these behaviors in ways that signal we understand our elders' frustrations and are eager to help.

Some Perspective: The Unique Communication Habits of Children

Let's get some perspective by looking at the communication habits of our children. What new parent doesn't burst with delight when an infant begins to babble? The constant repetition of the "da, da, das," and the "bah, bah, bahs" makes a young mother or father's heart sing! Never mind that six-month-old Susie calls every man she sees over the age of thirteen "da, da, da!" We think it's absolutely adorable and usually find ourselves responding in kind!

Take a common communication habit of our teenagers—verbal surliness ("Get out of my face!"). While unpleasant, this form of expression, we assume, is a necessary step they must take as they begin to define themselves as independent, mature adults.

While we go to great lengths to adapt to the communication style of children and accept that these language patterns are part of their normal development, we complain often about the communication habits of older adults and are less tolerant of their conversations. We see their habits as working against us, as oppositional and irritating. We ascribe their communication style to the diminished capacity that comes with aging. Comments like "she seems to be slowing down" and "he has a hard time sticking to the subject" are frequently heard from family members and professionals alike. With our children, we look for greater meaning in their communication patterns. But with older adults we assume there is less meaning, not more, and we bristle when they don't respond to our attempts to keep them on task and get things done. With our children we show creativity and patience; with older adults we tend to express frustration or concern.

This marked difference in attitude reflects a clear contrast in our assumptions about these age groups. We see children as exploring and assessing an unfolding and unfamiliar world. They are on a journey somewhere that requires new knowledge and skills. We give them ample room to be unfinished and rough around the edges. On the other hand, we see older adults as simply managing the familiar territory of adulthood with skills they've acquired over a lifetime. We don't look for anything beyond the literal meaning of what they say.

What we have failed to recognize, until now, is that seniors are on a journey that is exploring and assessing an unfamiliar world. They are leaving the familiarity of the task-driven middle-adult years and moving into the reflective and monumental terrain of their older years. They are replacing the drive to *do* with the drive to *weigh and measure;* "inside work" suddenly gains as much importance as "outside things." This uncharted journey gives rise to unique communication habits. Like those of growing children, these habits may appear unfinished and rough around the edges. On close inspection, we discover they reveal much more than we ever suspected.

This chapter looks at five verbal behaviors, quite common in older people, that may sound like mental decline, but quite possibly reveal something else.

Lack of Urgency
("Why can't they make a decision?")

Very often those who work with elderly people, or those who must interview them for a specific purpose, get exasperated and wonder, "Why can't they make a decision? I ask them a specific question and they don't seem to care about answering it. They aren't focused on the task at hand. I make decisions all the time—big ones, little ones. They aren't getting any younger and neither am I, yet they don't seem to be in any rush to resolve anything. What are they waiting for?"

Nowhere do we see the clash between age-based agendas more clearly than in the time it can take an older adult to decide something. This lack of urgency runs smack up against the deadlines our middle-aged agendas impose on us every day. We feel an uncontrollable urge to speed our elders up in an effort to satisfy our own internal agendas, not theirs. We share a culture of task orientation, embraced particularly by those of us who are juggling items on our midlife agendas. We measure our worth each day by how many faxes we receive and send, how many e-mail messages we blast off into cyberspace, how many dragons we metaphorically slay. And these older people can frustrate our attempts to surpass our previous day's output. We ask them a question and they won't give us an answer. Why can't they focus and respond?

Many senior adults understand that the landscape is more complicated once they slow down to take a good look at it. Compare their observation to our middle-aged agendas that drive us to rip through our lives with blinders on. Note that many middle-aged men do not appreciate the density of life's landscape until they have a heart attack. If they survive intensive care, the complexity and richness of living becomes apparent to them. Their physiology has forced them to slow down and they begin to look at their world in a different way. Similarly, as senior adults' physiology starts to slow down, they begin to focus on the internal and find that the life they've lived seventy years is complicated. This lack of urgency mirrors what's happening physiologically. Why can't they make a decision? Because making decisions is not what life is about. It isn't about quick sequencing. It's about understanding what has happened and what it all means.

For this reason, any attempt to create a sense of urgency in older adults is rarely successful and generally counterproductive. We are not talking about punctuality or efficiency. We are talking about the desire to light a fire under them to get them to take action. Unfortunately, most ploys to generate urgency simply ring false and older relatives and clients resent the tactic. Their resistance to being sped up comes from their enhanced perspective and says to us: We know something that you don't, that in the end, no matter how many phones calls we've returned, how many deals we've completed, how much money we've made, life always has a way of working out.

ONE seventy-nine-year-old woman I represented was being badgered—there's no other word for it—by her trusted advisors to change her will to conform to changes in the tax code, and she was resisting their pleas. The thrust of their argument was protection of her forty-nine-year-old son and his growing family from the ravages of estate taxes. As she pondered their explanation of a perfectly legal way to protect her assets, a junior partner decided to press for the close. Wouldn't it be a tragedy, he wondered out loud, if something happened before the plan could be implemented. The "something," left unspoken and hanging in the air, was an untimely change in her health, or perhaps her death. "What will your son do if you don't act and he's got to fork over all this money to the government?" he implored.

"No," said the woman seriously, quietly, thoughtfully. "He'll be okay. You know, he's a lot like his father. He's kind, he's smart, he's a good businessman, and a good father himself. Even if this [referring to her estate] were all taken away, he'd be just fine." It was a full six weeks before she got back in touch with her financial planner.

This client's enhanced perspective enabled her to resist the pressure to act quickly, supposedly to avoid an estate-planning disaster. What disaster could that be? Her answer mocked such an exaggeration. The issue, she insisted in her measured response, is not the money, as nice as it is, but rather the character of the person receiving it. Disaster or no disaster, she knew her son would be fine. No amount of rushing was going to change this important fact of life. She would take her time to decide if and when the plan would be implemented.

Exaggerated urgency aimed at older adults only makes them feel guilty and frustrated. Over the course of a lifetime, missed opportunities seem a minor, trivial concern at best. What matters is what we accomplished, not what we missed. No amount of rushing and doing makes life conform to the best-laid plans of its participants. Older people intuitively realize that life will always take care of itself.

Effective Communication Rules for Lack of Urgency

Accept the pace we see in older people as the normal end product of enhanced perspective.

- This simple strategy is also the most difficult to follow. We know they have gone farther up the mountain and are able to note that our somewhat exaggerated sense of urgency is no longer necessary for them. What we have to do is to integrate this perception into our behavior. We have to practice the art of acceptance. We have to make it the platform of a new attitude toward the unique dance of aging.

Don't take enhanced perspective personally.

- It has nothing to do with us. In working with older adults, especially our parents, it is hard *not* to take their resistance to our desire to move things along personally. This overlooked but important fact will help next time we feel the need to speed things up. Their enhanced perspective is at work whether we are pushing them or not.

- Practice the art of not taking it personally. Build on a new attitude that respects the older persons' pace by adding in an element of respectful detachment. Don't turn their journey into our personal grievance over their inability to move at our pace. We need to give ourselves the goal of being patient. Write it down. Review progress in thirty days. What worked? What didn't? Regroup and go for another thirty days. If we get discouraged, remember the way they were with us when we were dealing with the developmental issues of growing up. They were practicing then what we are trying to achieve now: patience.

Understand the difference between being punctual and being driven.

- Learn to be punctual without conditions. We need to manage our busy lives so we are not going to stop being organized or punctual. But many times we use punctuality as a vehicle to speed up older adults. Practice a form of punctuality that can incorporate the fact that original plans are always subject to last-minute changes.

- Use punctuality as a vehicle to return control to the older person. We need to use language that offers a partnership in preserving punctuality but leaves the final decision to the older person. "If you want that errand done by three p.m., I will make sure I have the car around front by two-thirty p.m." "If you want to visit him next month, I'll make sure I can get time off from work."

Become expert at spontaneous facilitation.

- Display facilitation skills at the right moment. In our middle adult years we use task-driven facilitation skills that make us productive and have their place. Once senior adults' agendas accelerate, we may need to apply these skills on a moment's notice.

■ Practice the art of rapid gear changes. In the case of parents, isn't that what they did for us—quickly change gears—when our developmental agenda spiked? Without consulting them, it drove us to creep, crawl, walk, and dispense with those babyish training wheels—and forced them to get creative about how to deal with these changes. We need that same attitude now, which is accepting the fact that there are going to be some spikes in Dad's agenda that will accelerate the game plan and only then will I move quickly to help out. Once their agenda changes, we can fully engage our midlife task-driven, sequencing skills.

If we can understand and accept this timeline produced by enhanced perspective, then we can derive great satisfaction by exercising our deadline-driven skills at the appropriate time. Rather than insist the elderly person get something done, let the impetus come from the elderly person. Letting them lead is the way to deal with lack of urgency and feel good about it.

Predictable Encounters

Predictable Encounters is a practical application section that illustrates how we might use information in the chapter to bridge communication difficulties with our elders. We focus on discerning senior adults' unique communication habits and learning to respond appropriately, that is, according to their age-based agenda, not ours.

Predictable Encounter: Lack of Urgency

In the next thirty days, identify one situation in which your need to get something done is at odds with an older adult's timing. Describe the situation and your reasons for the urgency. Are there less urgent alternatives to speeding up the older adult?

Example: Your mother has not made an appointment for her follow-up visit with her doctor. Her medication is running out and she must have a checkup before her prescriptions can be refilled. You are tempted to get aggressive on this issue and make the appointment for her, but you fear a negative reaction that might further delay her seeking proper treatment.

Questions: What alternatives are there to taking this step? Which offer her the control she needs in this situation?

Possible answers: (1) Call the physician's office and find out what times are available in the next week. Tell your mother about these open appointments. (2) Offer her the option of making the appointment or having you make the appointment for her.

How to Say It:

"Mom, I've checked with Dr. Reed's office and his appointment book is filling up. Do you want me to schedule your check up or shall I let you handle it?"

Nonlinear Conversations
("Why can't they stick to the subject?")

Not only do older adults move slowly when viewed from our younger vantage point, they also have the habit of wandering off the topic of conversation, which we sometimes find annoying. In children we label this behavior as being "off task." With older adults some have labeled it "off-topic speech" or "off-topic verbosity." While children are given leeway to operate off task, we expect our older citizens to know better and act accordingly. When older adults drift from the topic, we assume the cause is the infirmity of their advancing years. What else could it be?

As Rabbi Schachter-Shalomi points out in *From Age-ing to Sage-ing,* aging demands that we stop rushing and conquering and begin to search for the pattern of what's happened in our lives. Whether we like it or not, there is no sequence to that process. It's not neat, and it takes time. Nonlinear conversations can jump-start or accelerate that process by opening doors to subjects that otherwise would never be mentioned.

I once had to evaluate a San Francisco matriarch whose husband died and left her in charge of a multibillion-dollar fortune. She was reportedly short-tempered, haughty, and dismissive of any fool who crossed her path, which included just about everyone she encountered. None of her financial advisors had ever been able to spend more than about fifteen minutes with her at one time, because she quickly tired of their "plans" and their "games" about what to do with her wealth. I was advised to prepare in advance and focus my questions to make the most of that quarter hour she might put up with me. But some instinct told me to take the opposite approach. Instead of hitting her with facts and figures and a predetermined strategy, I began with an open-ended question (see chapter 10), "Tell me about yourself."

She looked amazed. "From the *beginning?*" she asked, incredulously.

"Yes, from the very beginning."

And for the next two and a half hours, despite several not-so-discreet reminders from a bevy of assistants hired to keep her on schedule, I listened to the story of this woman's life in great detail. When she talked about her coming-out party, her face glowed like the debutante she once was. She told me about her courtship, her wedding day, her life as a Northern California art patron. I noticed she skipped over her children, a hiccup in an otherwise detailed conversation that told me something important was underneath. I decided not to press her for details, although I thought it odd that she wouldn't mention the subject. I heard that hiccup more than once and then a curious nonlinear remark: "You know, doctors don't know everything. Mothers do." And what followed was a lengthy account of the certain knowledge she had that something was wrong with her fourth pregnancy, but which her doctors assured her was "all in her head." But she was correct, and when this baby arrived as what we now call a special-needs child, the charmed existence she had known was over.

WE have to create an environment for nonlinear conversations by signaling we're willing to listen, and that we're tuned in to the content, not just the words, of the conversation we're hearing. If we are in a professional setting and encounter an elderly person who engages in this form of verbal behavior, how should we respond? Simply listen. By listening for the patterns in any nonlinear conversation, it's possible we might help someone discover something important about how he or she wants to be remembered.

Why do we find nonlinear conversations so frustrating? We are an over-stimulated generation, much more comfortable with the *Reader's Digest* version of everything. Sometimes we feel as if we've exceeded our genetic tasking capacity by a factor of five. What this density of tasking produces is so much overstimulation that we get depressed, because the job we have chosen was never one we were wired to do. As we keep sequencing more and more tightly, we think we'll be able to manage everything, but it's not true. We simply run out of patience for anyone or anything that gets in our way. It is no wonder we display minimal empathy for older adults who go off on tangents. How inefficient, we think. And we would be correct if sequential task completion were a primary need of aging. It turns out it is not. True, seniors have things that need to be done, but these missions have less to do with rapid-fire task completion and more to do with recognizing the significance of life's events.

Upon closer observation, nonlinear conversations serve an important role in the life-review process of older adults. They are a tool the elderly use—consciously or subconsciously—to find purpose, direction, and meaning from what they've experienced. What emerges from these nonlinear conversations are personal stories that reflect core values and central themes in a life lived over seventy or eighty years. This discovery process amasses the raw data that will be used to define that life and its legacy. It is important to remember that in many cases this discovery process is not what older adults have in mind when they begin a conversation.

Nonlinear conversations, if given ample support, can lead to great insight. Conversations that flow and evolve at their own pace emphasize values that carry special meaning for the older person. A nonlinear conversation can express these values in either a positive or negative context. Many such conversations I have had with older adults led to recollections of betrayal, dishonesty, greed, and lost love. In these cases the patterns that emerge highlight goals that were cherished, but not fulfilled, or were left unrealized or overtly ignored. Such lessons are no less meaningful or admired in the life-review process than stories about success. In fact, the most significant lessons are sometimes taught where the values fail to be realized. As one older client said about finally understanding her parents, "Sometimes we seem to back into the truth."

Effective Communication Rules for Nonlinear Conversations

View nonlinear conversations as a sorting, discovery, and remediation tool.

- Practice striking a balance between listening to and facilitating non-linear conversations. As we will see in later chapters, posing the right question can mean all the difference in our ability to successfully start or follow up a nonlinear conversation. We can't be passive when we hear these conversations, because they are too important. We must respond to them for developmental growth in our elders to occur, the way they responded to us to promote such growth in our childhoods.

Nonlinear conversations can produce spontaneous revelations and insights.

- Commit to creating opportunities for spontaneous revelations. Life is more than a list of to-do items. Relax. Let the conversation define itself. Intentionally introduce nonlinear moments. Set this process in motion, facilitate it, and then give it room to breathe.

- Be prepared for the big one. Once nonlinear conversation begins to flow, a topic may emerge that makes the difference between a life that comes to completion through legacy and one left hanging in the balance.

In a study published in *Pomona College Magazine,* researcher Deborah Burke, who has studied aging and cognition for more than twenty years, commented on the effects of aging on retention of language skills. She noted that elderly people usually go off task when presenting personal narratives, and those narratives move toward issues with high moral significance. We need to appreciate that nonlinear conversations revisit essential chapters and themes of a life. Understood in that context, what the elderly are doing is not surprising: They are revisiting past conflicts. These conflicts resurface because they are turning points in the person's life: the losses, changes, peaks, and successes. We become like whale watchers. We know as we listen to non-linear conversations that something significant is going to surface. We just don't know when.

Nonlinear conversations are a vehicle for revisiting the life dramas that test and clarify values.

- Not all life dramas have happy endings. Regrets, loss, conflict, and tragedy all occupy the human experience as much as accomplishments, gains, friendships, and love realized. When people revisit their lives, they find both the comedy and tragedy. Seniors need opportunities to gauge and weigh their lives.

- See the emerging dramas as a measure of the players and their values. In these conversations, the older person's values are tested, clarified, and reconfirmed. The past event may have been a tragedy, but values were clarified because of that tragedy and have proved to be solid, noteworthy, and correct.

Nonlinear conversations are closely related to the next communication repetition, probably the most common and one experienced by anyone who has ever spent a significant amount of time in the company of an older adult.

Predictable Encounter: Nonlinear Conversation

In the next thirty days, identify a nonlinear conversation with an older person. Note the starting point and the natural thread of the conversation.

Example: You run into one of your older neighbors and ask how she's doing. Her reply is a monologue that twists through past and present events and far exceeds the time you mentally allotted for the entire conversation.

Questions: How do you respond to such a complex answer to a simple question without being offensive or dismissive?

Possible Answers: Our midlife agenda would naturally drive us to cut this kind of conversation short. Instead of trying to control the conversation or somehow slither out of it, respond to it in the following way:

1. Listen for patterns and themes. Is this a tale about perseverance, cleverness, irony, or life's difficulties? Try to identify a theme and then, if you can, paraphrase or summarize the lesson or moral significance of what the person is saying.

How to Say It:

"It seems to me, in life, things that should be simple turn out to be complicated. Isn't it amazing that you start out with good intentions and everything backfires on you."

Echo back to this woman the values she expresses in her verbal labyrinth.

2.   Tell a similar story from your own life.

How to Say It:

"This sounds very much like the time I was dealing with my mom when she was really ill. . . ."

By echoing what you've heard, you show you're listening and you get to summarize the meaning. Your version may facilitate her understanding of her story's importance.

Repetition
("Why do they always tell that same boring story?")

We may have heard Grandma's story about the night she met Grandpa close to a hundred times, and think she's becoming senile. Yet there may be a reason for the repetition that has nothing to do with mental decline: There's something in that incident, like the patterns discovered in nonlinear conversations, that recalls a moment of exceptional value in her life. She is repeating that story as part of her life-review process. Our job is to listen in ways that help her discover what it is about that encounter that needs to become part of her legacy.

In his book *The Force of Character,* James Hillman argues that repetition by older adults reveals the character of the "characters" in their stories. Hillman's story about a garrulous uncle triggered a memory about a disastrous experience with one of my own uncles. Unlike the uncle in Hillman's story, my uncle was a prince of a man who taught me, eventually, one of life's most important lessons: It's all about what you value.

I cringe every time I think of my own experience with my dear old Uncle Albert when I was at the height of my adolescent-arrogant phase. It illustrates many of the ways that we react to old people and they react to us. We've all been teenagers, so we have experienced that time in life when we think we're hot stuff but are in fact pathetically insufferable. I was like this for weeks when I was about fourteen years old, so much so that my family contemplated shipping me out of state until I came to my senses. This phase culminated one day at my grandmother's house when my uncle began to tell the same story he'd been repeating for years in what I thought at the time was excruciatingly boring detail.

So on this day at the height of my adolescent horridness, I interrupted Uncle Albert just as he began telling his story and proceeded to finish it for him, in rapid summary, in front of the entire family. If that weren't enough and oblivious to the reaction of my other relatives, I then faced him and said, "Uncle Albert, why do you always tell that same boring story?" And my Uncle Albert—an incredibly sweet, angelic man—looked at me and said simply, "It's a good story." It took me thirty years to figure out what he was really saying.

What was the story? During the Depression, my uncle and his two older brothers were living on a farm on the outskirts of Minneapolis, and they had no paychecks. It was a very bad time—they had no income, were barely eating, and could not afford to meet the payments on their property. One day a man in Minneapolis offered one of them a job that, if advertised today, might not see an applicant for decades: chipping ice off railroad tracks at 3 a.m. in weather that approached thirty below. The ice had to be chipped off the tracks before trains could start arriving at the railroad station. The salary: $7.50 per week! The three brothers went down to the railroad station and begged the guy to hire all three of them, at $2.50 per week each. They needed to tell people that they were employed. As Albert told the story, the railroad official agreed and those three brothers could never remember whose turn it was to get up and chip that ice. I have this image, from the many times I heard its recounting, of the three of them meeting in the kitchen early on a bitter cold morning and acting like the Three Stooges: "I'll go." "No, it's my turn to go." "No, no, I'll go." "Oh heck, let's all go!"

Now, thirty years later, I can tell you: That is a *great* story. About what? About loyalty. About love. About self-respect. About how a family confronts hardship and sticks together. Powerful stuff. His brothers were long dead, yet Albert still loved telling that story.

Albert didn't repeat that story because he was old or demented or mentally deficient. He repeated it because telling that story allowed him to revisit events in his life that possessed exceptional value—and are in large part what made him who he thought himself to be: a man who values work, loyalty, family, and love.

We take repetition as some sort of deficiency of aging, as a sign that older people are starting to slip. But in fact this communication habit is a powerful and necessary part of their life-review process by which they begin to piece together their organic legacy. Repeating stories allows them to line up those events that had enormous impact on defining who they are and how they view the world. The repeated facts are not important, it's the *values* those facts represent that allow senior adults to tap into the opportunity to recontextualize their very being and begin to form their legacy. In chapter 10 we'll address specific strategies that enable us to recognize—and respond to—the values in any conversation.

Repetition is not an inward drift to the past coupled with less interest in or disengagement from the present. It is part of the great sorting process necessary for life review. If nonlinear communication focuses on people and events that carry exceptional value, repetition gives those values deeper definition.

Effective Communication Rules for Repetition

Pay attention, when you hear a story being repeated, to what is being emphasized.

- Seek to mentally weigh the purpose of the story. Where is the person putting primary emphasis? On the content, the drama, the values of a story? All three? What or who is being drawn into focus? Sum up in a phrase the message of the story being retold. Perseverance? Betrayal? Loyalty? Self-indulgence? Self-sacrifice?

Understand that repetition is a form of emphasis.

- Learn to separate the wheat from the chaff. Repetition doesn't point to something that is completely developed in the person's thinking or feeling about his or her life. It may point to something that needs more work, further enhancement, or clarification.

- Take mental notes on the wheat. As items surface through repetition, take notes on their topics and who is involved. These topics will prove invaluable later on as we compose enhancement and clarification sentences.

Be aware that repetition may be a kind of obstruction to the sorting process; the nonlinear, conscious, or unconscious search has been done, but its significance is not yet understood. Uncle Albert's response to teenage me— "It's a good story"—may signal his limited understanding of the story's significance in his life review or (probably in his case) his certainty that the story's significance would be meaningless to a fifteen-year-old.

Even if the significance of a repeated story is understood, its role in the organic legacy may remain a mystery.

- The ending may be a surprise to everyone. Even the familiar can surprise in terms of what it finally means. Many important stories require further retelling to mine some useful insight into a form that makes sense to the elderly person's life review.

At all stages of life we repeat stories: to brag, to clarify or resolve a problem, or to amuse. When we hear an older person repeat a story, however, we need to listen with a different set of ears, for the repetition can contain useful information about the person's struggle with the life-review process. We aren't necessarily appreciating a repeated story's full implication, which may or may not be obvious to the storyteller. We may need to develop questions that will facilitate or help clarify the story to the person. With further development, more information is revealed and the themes and values can be repackaged to shape the person's organic legacy.

Predictable Encounter: Repetition

The Predictable Encounter for repetition sends us back into our own child-hoods but works toward the same understanding of an older person's developmental tasks and communication methods.

Example: You also have an "Uncle Albert" who repeats family stories and you don't know how to respond. Think back to your childhood and the stories you heard from him and other family members. Focus on one story and try to recall the first time you heard it. Remember as much detail as you can about that story. Then, identify the main theme(s) of the story.

Questions: Was this story a turning point in your loved one's life? A celebration of love or friendship? An inevitable tragedy? The closing of one of life's chapters? What values were championed, admired, or represented by the story? Are these the values you associate with the storyteller today? If that person has passed on, would you say these values are part of his or her legacy? If so, in what way are these values expressed? Through the younger generation? Through writings? Through the person's religious association? How do you incorporate those values in your own life?

Possible Answers: The next time you hear an elderly person repeat a story, highlight the story's values by asking for clarification or offering a personal anecdote of your own that expresses those values.

How to Say It:

"Your story always makes me wish my life were less hectic. What do you think I'm missing today that was so important then?"

"I know what you mean by the rush of technology. The new hires in my office know how to operate the latest gadgets before the IS department issues instructions."

These kinds of responses will help the storyteller clarify his reasons for the repetition and quite possibly lead to an epiphany regarding legacy.

*   *   *

IN thinking about a repeated story you heard from a relative who has passed away, try to see the connection between the values in that story and the person. If you can't make such a connection, think about why these values didn't surface during the person's lifetime. One possible reason is that no one acknowledged the repetition in a way that enabled values to emerge.

Attention to Details
("Why do they fret so much about the unimportant stuff?")

My relationship with my mother began to improve after my father's death because I learned how to signal her that I was truly available to listen. I had learned at long last that my most important job from her point of view was to listen and help her figure out the important themes and events in her life. I wasn't listening so much for content as I was for patterns. When I signaled I was focused and up to the task, I heard about my mother's life in a way I never had before.

One afternoon I had three hours after an appointment in my hometown of Portland, Oregon, before leaving for the airport, so I called my mom and asked her to meet me at a Starbucks. And instead of checking my watch every five minutes and looking my usual impatient self, I turned off my cell phone and pager, sat back, and indicated with my focused gaze and relaxed body language that I had nothing more important to do that afternoon than to converse with her. And after about twenty minutes—I had not said anything—she started to tell a story I'd heard many times, but this time, she revealed details I'd never heard before: "You know, after Myrtle died, my life changed. I was never the same person again."

I knew that my Aunt Myrtle had drowned when she was nineteen and my mom was ten, and that it was a significant event not much talked about in the family. But never had Mom told me this story the way she did that afternoon. As I listened to all the details, she revealed that moment in her life when time stood still.

She went on to paint a picture and fill it with people—what they said, what they wore, how they reacted—that meant the most to her. I can tell you how Myrtle's hair was cut, what her boyfriend looked like, the color of the T-shirt he wore, the model of car he drove, her friends, my great-grandmother's kitchen. I can tell you every nuance of that young lady's life the last time my mother saw her. This was *not* a story about how life always works out. This is a story about how it sometimes betrays us. But even the betrayals reflect what she values: loyalty, family, connection. In this instance, life didn't provide any of that.

Instead of trying to rush the details, we might ask why these details are so intense. And the answer is, at the end of life, seniors rev up the landscape in an attempt to determine what's most important. Through this process they are saying, I remember these details; they are a part of who I am.

When we hear lots of details in repeated stories, we note that the storyteller's version may not be exactly correct, the way *we* remember the incident, or the way the person related an earlier version of the same story. So we may find ourselves commenting that this older person's memory is slipping, or isn't exactly correct as we remember it. But *correct* is not the deal here. They are not scripting a documentary. They're using memory as a vehicle with which to intensify a part of their life that means a lot to them. They're reaching for a value. They're trying to understand a person. Attention to detail is one way to get there.

Effective Communication Rules for Attention to Details

Appreciate the details and listen to them carefully.

- Teach yourself not to prematurely dismiss familiar stories or themes. A change in details can rewrite the meaning of even the most familiar story. Tuning out what seems familiar may cause us to miss a crucial plot change in a life story.

- Practice seeing the landscape in color. Appreciate that, like repetition, details operate as a vehicle for creating depth, not unlike colorizing black-and-white footage.

When listening to the details, get inside the scene the older person is describing.

- See the details as a novelist. The novelist seeks the reader's engagement to bring a story to life. Engagement is essential to connection. Older adults seek the same thing. They are connecting to the past and the present through nonlinear screening, repetition, and enhancement with details. Not the devil, but the stuff of life lived is found in the details. Life review uses the same building blocks. While some details may seem trivial or insignificant, we need consistent engagement to recognize when significance starts to surface. That's how we can learn what's important to that person.

Be alert to the values that may not be obvious amidst the details.

■ Learn to notice the implied values. For instance, a person may go on at length about another person's manner of dress, giving us a subtle clue that the speaker values appearance. Some details may reveal evidence of personal sacrifice and whether self-sacrifice is valued or not. Note details about a point in life where someone felt secure, one of those glorious peak moments where everything was working out. Know that these moments may be important in building a legacy.

Don't assume details contain hidden commands.

■ Details don't mandate any action on our part. Lots of details we hear may be quite painful and we assume we're being asked to solve something, when in fact all we are required to do is listen. We'll gain a lot more valuable information about what the person values through listening than through acting.

Listen for details that reveal: What's the message here? What's really being valued? Are the details drawing us into a drama that asks us to relive or reexperience a person or event?

Details are not a prompt for action; they're the tools an elderly person applies to life's landscape as a painter applies color to a canvas: to see something through a different light, different time, different perspective. Little by little the complete picture emerges.

Predictable Encounter: Attention to Details

Below is an attempt to discern the significance amidst the verbiage.

Example: Your elderly Aunt Thelma has been housebound for years, but today insists she needs a new pair of shoes. She's been requesting this same shoe roughly twice a year for eons; nevertheless she describes exactly what she wants—brand, style, size, and color. On this occasion you discover, to your dismay, that the style has been discontinued. You find substitutes, but she rejects every pair you bring for her inspection. She won't even try the merchandise on: She knows by merely lifting the shoe ("Too heavy!") out of the box that your dozen purchases must all be returned.

Question: Although you love her, this woman has never been easy to deal with and you know she won't let this shoe issue go away. What's the best way to handle this situation?

Possible Answers: Although she may not be able to express it, your aunt probably cares about connection with you more than she cares about the shoes. Fussing about the size, style, weight, and price of a pair of shoes is her way of controlling the daily tasks of living she was once able to perform for herself. Beyond her need for control, whether she expresses it or not, is her need for your attention in whatever form she can get it: shopping, discussing, returning, then starting the process all over again.

Her focus on shoes, though, may provide a clue to opening up a discussion much more relevant to her end-of-life tasks.

How to Say It:
"Aunt Thelma, I'm curious. How old were you when you bought your first pair of high heels?"

Responding to her interest in shoe details may open a door she'll leap through to focus on events much closer to her heart. Don't tune out the details; probe them instead.

Uncoupling
("Was it something I said?")

Uncoupling is a nice term that implies we didn't quite hit the mark and therefore the person with whom we're trying to communicate has disconnected from us, usually for "inexplicable" reasons. This communication habit is particularly frustrating for professionals who work with older people. Just when we are so sure we are right on course, we wind up being dismissed or ignored. Uncoupling is difficult because at the heart of it is rejection, something no one wants to face.

Remember the mogul and his thirty-something son with the ponytail, whom we met in an earlier chapter? Remember that his advisors came up with Mr. Ponytail as the mogul's legacy, but Mr. Ponytail didn't work? As his advisors were reviewing his portfolios, the mogul was reviewing his life—and struggling to come up with some meaning to it. When they failed, he uncoupled, much to the frustration of his advisors. "I'll get back to you" is the kiss of death to a professional whose midlife agenda requires a daily quota of slain dragons. Uncoupling happens, in many instances, when there's a disconnect between two age-based agendas. We may think helping an older person discover his legacy is all about time and money, that what we need to do to create a legacy is finance a project or an idea that furthers a person's interests. That approach works sometimes, but only if we're able to uncover something that the person finds meaningful. When we hear older adults disengage, we can be sure that we haven't touched their legacy issues. Knowing a need exists is half the information battle. The other half is achieving real communication by using language that connects with their notion of who they are.

It's important to look at uncoupling as a useful marker. Accept it as a signal that we need more information from the archives of the person's life. We may be on target with our goal, but the strategy or style or technique or package isn't quite right. We need to extend our thinking and modify our approach to reach that person. We need to rethink our approach and decide if it's working for us or against us.

A friend, Bob, told me a story recently that illustrates this point about uncoupling. He and his sister had been trying to get their mother to move into assisted living for years. She seemed open to the idea, but insisted she wanted to remain in Chicago even though both her children lived far away and hoped she'd choose to live near either one of them. Bob dutifully did his research and came up with several attractive options he thought his mom would like, but every time he presented options, she refused to discuss the matter. Thinking he hadn't hit upon the right situation for her, he did more research and tried to propose more choices, yet whenever he aired the subject, she shrugged him off. He decided he needed to change his approach, so he one day asked an open-ended question instead (see chapter 10): "Mom, if you could live anywhere, where would that be?" She hesitated (perhaps indicating that life review was underway), then uttered an answer that astonished him: "In Florida. Close to your sister."

Both he and his sister had suggested Florida many times, but their mom never considered it. He commented to me that he felt angry at her for all the time he'd wasted, but he resisted an initial impulse that would have made her feel bad. Instead, he asked why living near her daughter was so important.

"I want to be close to my grandchildren." Why hadn't she expressed that wish months earlier? "Because I don't want to be a burden." When she understood that it was *more* of a burden to both children for her to live so far away, she felt comfortable with her decision and graciously accepted the help she needed to make the move. Bob would never have unearthed this wish if he'd ignored the message she was sending by uncoupling. If he'd stayed the course with his well-researched plan, he would never have asked the question that led his mother to the heartfelt answer.

The lesson here is that legacy—in this case Bob's mother's desire to be valued as Grandma and maintain close family ties—is not something the elderly can always articulate, although they keep trying. Appreciating the items on their agenda can save a lot of time. When we approach what's close to their heart, when they begin to see their path through the haze of accumulated experience, their entire demeanor changes. Rather than uncouple, they can make a decision instantly.

Uncoupling requires a bit more persistence on our part, not to fulfill our agendas but to facilitate theirs. Wisdom, intuition, persistence, and patience are needed.

Effective Communication Rules for Uncoupling

Uncoupling is not fatal.

- Learn from failed attempts. Uncoupling is a necessary blip in the process that indicates we need to go back and assess the quality of the information we've gathered. If we're sure our information is sound, then we need to look at ways to repackage it. If it's packaged well, look at ways to re-communicate it or re-present it. Our connection isn't over; it needs some fine-tuning.

Rethink the objective.

▪ Be clear about what is not working. Many times we think we know what the older person's drivers are and we want to score a goal (closure of a deal, for instance). We need to remind ourselves that our midlife agenda is not the point here; the focus is how the older person wishes to be remembered. Don't forget the two main issues an elderly person is dealing with: maintaining control and discovering a legacy. Any action or communication that works against those purposes will produce uncoupling.

Uncoupling is not a hang up, it's a disconnect.

▪ Be committed to redialing. When the lines get disconnected, there's almost always another chance to reestablish that connection. In fact, elderly people can be very patient in this respect. We get lots of chances to start over by asking different questions, posing the same queries in a different way, and giving the person ample room to answer.

Predictable Encounter: Uncoupling

Uncoupling is a disconnect, not a dismissal. Here's how to reestablish a direct line.

Example: There are two subjects that pique your curiosity, but about which your father is reticent: what he did during World War II and what life was like when he was a boy. Whenever you broach these topics, he dismisses you with statements like "It's a closed chapter. Let's not go there," or "Why do you want all this useless information?"

Questions: Should you pursue such discussions? If so, what verbal cues or behavior strategies can be used to unlock the knowledge from his vast memory stores?

Possible Answers: In addition to the familiar age-based agenda clashes, there is a sociocultural difference at work here. Your father's generation went through difficult years, yet always looked forward to better times and rarely looked back. From his parents he was handed a big "no whining" sticker at birth and was programmed to stand up to adversity and press on.

Given these generational differences, sometimes it's best not to press for information. Your elderly relative will *not* forget your request, but may need time to gather thoughts together.

Most elderly people will eventually want to talk about their parents' generation and their own childhoods, however. Continue to offer open-ended questions (see chapter 10) and be aware that, in your next interaction, the elderly person might drop subtle conversational clues that he or she is now ready to discuss these previously difficult subjects.

How else to reconnect? Begin with a self-revelation. Talk about your earliest memory and then ask the older person about the same subject. You'll learn a lot and begin to mine layers of experience that cloud the ability to discover legacy. Many times when there's hesitancy to offer information, the only way to begin the conversation is to offer some information about yourself, then ask the question to which you want answers.

How to Say It:

"Dad, I avoided military service by staying in school. Now my sons want to enlist and we're at war. What do you think I should tell them?"

"Dad, I remember your Uncle Joe from my childhood, but I don't know where he fits on our family tree. Would you help me figure it out?"

These kinds of questions offer senior adults the role that our modern culture and hectic lifestyle have denied them—that of the wise, experienced head of the clan with knowledge and wisdom to impart. If sincerely asked, these questions can open up subjects that lead to revelations by which our elders will be remembered and which may become part of our own legacies.

By redefining senior adults' communication habits as a set of tools they use to tackle end-of-life tasks, we begin to see these habits not as annoying or frustrating or a sign of decline, but as keys that facilitate their developmental mission. We don't punish a toddler for having a meltdown in the grocery store; similarly, as we appreciate the developmental tasks the elderly face, we can view these communication habits, not as deficits, but as their way of getting the job done. Redefining these habits as tools gives them a kind of dignity and augments our appreciation of an elderly person's enormous end-of-life journey. This appreciation allows us to be more patient and creative in our approach to the elderly people in our lives.

THE next chapter examines the way the world looks from an elderly person's viewpoint, the common issues they face. Understanding these issues grounds us in their reality and expands our ability to communicate without experiencing the frustration our midlife agendas might otherwise impose.

SIX

The Predictable Dilemmas
of Getting Old

"The solution of every problem is another problem."

—*Johann Wolfgang von Goethe*

OLD age presents our elders with a formidable landscape. This chapter presents five predictable dilemmas the elderly face and offers suggestions about how we can help them minimize frustration and maximize opportunities to resolve the conflicting items on their age-based agendas. The five predictable dilemmas are the following:

- Where will I live?

- How can I best manage my health?

- How will I cope all by myself?

- What should I do about money?

- What is the right way to say good-bye?

These predictable dilemmas of aging are real-life situations that can be sources of difficulty for our elders and potential conflict between generations. We explore how seniors tend to react, how we typically respond, and how a legacy coach might help. Specifically we come to understand:

- how senior adults experience this world and respond to its complexities;

- how society frustrates their ability to navigate these dilemmas themselves;

- how we can step up to the plate and coach them through these trying events.

This chapter addresses the world of senior adults from a vantage point we have yet to attain. It offers strategies and skills to help the elderly communicate, explore, cope, and thrive in an environment that is sometimes hostile to their needs. Our aim is to give senior adults the support they need to focus on their end-of-life tasks. If we are successful, we are rewarded in ways that not only minimize our mutual frustration but also make real communication possible, pleasurable, and instructive.

Nurturing the Elderly

The elderly people I meet through my work are in compromised health, yet usually need to obtain life-insurance policies to complete their estate planning. My job, as I mentioned in the introduction to this book, is to figure out, based on their medical history and current health status, how long they'll live. Life expectancy determines if they are insurable and what price they'll need to pay for coverage. But how do you determine how long an older adult might live?

In working with older clients, I found that exploring both medical and psychological factors is key to arguing for the most optimistic life expectancy. How long someone may live is a matter of past health as well as his or her current medical condition. But the mortality of older adults also has a psychological component that is referred to as *functional ability*. Functional ability tells us how older adults operate physically and psychologically. In many cases their psychological health is the stronger of the two predictors. I have come to realize that, in my role as my company's medical director, I am more than a physician's assistant (PA) who assesses blood pressure, EKGs, and hospital reports. In many cases, I am the first person to perform a true legacy checkup.

I developed the role of legacy coach, who weighs and measures the progress of potential clients as they sort out their end-of-life tasks, because I found great reluctance by family members and professionals to ask the profound questions that lead to life review. But in assessing life expectancy, such questions naturally arise and I don't hesitate to ask them: How has your life been different from your parents? At this point, what is your perception of your life's meaning? How would you like to be remembered and by whom? Judging from the thoughtful responses I get, I am convinced these issues are on the developmental front burner of almost every older client I have represented. There are very few cases where an important insight, discussion, or decision did not come to light as I performed a legacy checkup. I soon realized that the difference between my success or failure as a legacy coach had nothing to do with the senior I was evaluating. It had everything to do with me and my skills.

I also discovered that being a legacy coach involves many of the same skills that parents employ in raising their children. As parents, we guide our children through each developmental phase on their way to adulthood and recognize the phases as part of their normal growth pattern. When physical growth is over, we become more of a mentor or friend, the same role that we assume as a legacy coach for an elderly person. As legacy coach, we must intervene in the older person's two big developmental issues; that intervention takes the form of running interference from overwhelming invasion in the wars for control, and recognizing the internal struggle that ensues in the life-review process. If we are successful in these two missions, then the older person has the chance to focus on legacy and feel as though his or her life is transformed. Without legacy coaches, our elders are in danger of becoming developmental orphans.

Becoming a Legacy Coach

Part of this book's purpose is to illustrate how to become expert legacy coaches. We've already taken a big step by understanding the communication habits of the elderly that can signal the conflict they feel between their need for control and their need to let go; the rest of this book offers practical suggestions and skills that can facilitate resolution of this conflict and lead to life review. These skills are easy to learn and effective with any elderly person with whom we come into contact—relative, patient, client, friend, or acquaintance. Once learned, they are always at our command and transferable; we won't lose the ability to pass them along to the younger generation in the discovery of our own legacies when the time comes.

Briefly, the primary job of legacy coaches is to help senior adults discover the ways they wish to be remembered. To accomplish this enormous task, legacy coaches do the following:

- Understand the items on senior adults' age-based agenda and the ways they express the conflict they feel;

- Ensure that their control issues are managed;

- Ask them meaningful questions that prompt life review;

- Listen attentively and reinforce the values contained in their answers;

- Facilitate the predictable life dilemmas seniors face, as discussed below.

Why do we need to become legacy coaches? Because in aiding the elderly in their battles for control and allowing them to focus on defining their legacy, we ourselves become transformed. Without needless battles for control, we benefit from the insights and wisdom they arrive at in uncovering legacy. In the process we are able to give more of ourselves and get more in return. Like the teacher at his retirement party who swears he received more from his students than he ever gave to them, many people have told me they reap personal benefits as the legacy of someone dear unfolds. As we read about the predictable life dilemmas seniors face, we begin to understand how we can acquire the skills needed to help them cope.

Predictable Dilemma 1: Where Will I Live?

Many baby boomers have faced the challenge illustrated in previous chapters. Mom and Dad, now in their seventies, are no longer able to maintain the home in which they raised their family. But when we broach the subject of moving to a retirement home or assisted-living facility, our parents refuse to discuss the topic. On the subject of where they will live, the elderly frequently dig in their heels.

> *Their Predictable Reaction:* "Here is just fine."
> *Our Predictable Response:* "You're not serious?"

Given the developmental agenda driving *us,* we argue, cajole, and try to persuade our elders that moving is "for their own good." There are safety issues or practical financial considerations. After all, who is going to put up those storm windows, regrout the bathtub, or shop for groceries when they are no longer able to drive? On a fixed income, how will they be able to pay for unexpected major repairs that houses need from time to time—replacing the roof or repaving the driveway—we want to know. An assisted-living facility makes so much sense: Someone else does building maintenance; provides round-the-clock medical assistance; cooks a hot meal every day. There is usually a social director to supervise activities. They'll be with their peer group. We've researched the subject and the advantages are attractive and undeniable. How can they not see the wisdom of selling the house to a growing young family that needs the space and can enjoy it in ways that have become a burden to our elders and to us?

Legacy Coach's Approach

Be aware of the role the family home plays as the memory repository necessary for many senior adults' life review. We need to respect their decision and refocus our energies.

STEP UP TO THE PLATE

If their health permits, consider getting them the support services they need in order to remain in their home. If we are going to get pushy, let's push for better home-care services. If they need help with house maintenance, we must find someone to do the work. Call Meals On Wheels to make sure they have a hot meal every day. Be sure they have transportation to whatever church, community group, or recreational facility they're interested in attending so they won't feel isolated. Make it clear by our actions that they can stay in their home as long as they want.

USE THE PLANT-AND-WAIT TECHNIQUE

In this situation, the plant-and-wait technique works well. When we sense resistance to the idea of moving, drop the subject entirely and instead bring the house to life. Reconstruct stories, events, passages, and themes from their life in the house. We need to allow them to repeat stories we may have heard many times, but now listen with our legacy-coach ears and respond, not with boredom but with renewed interest. Ask them what first attracted them to the home. Ask them about a detail of the story that may have changed from the last time we heard it. If we share our own memories of particular incidents, allow them to refine our impressions. Ask them questions about their life in the house after the children left. Such questions unlock a flood of memories they need to process and factor into the web of their legacy.

Don't mention moving until *they* bring up the subject again. And they will, because once they have done the psychic sorting they need to do and the home's meaning to their legacy is clear, their need for connection with the physical space will disappear. They'll begin to ask subtle questions such as "Is that new block of apartments completed?" "How has the economic downturn affected rents in our area?" "Dad and I would love to take a ride and look at that place you were interested in a while ago."

As legacy coaches, we must realize that the question "Where will I live?" gives us the opportunity to explore both control and legacy issues and take advantage of the legacy density that the family home offers. If we don't, we're missing an opportunity to help our elders explore a vital piece of the reflective work they need to do as they near the end of their lives.

How to Say It:

The answer to the question "Where will I live?" is

> *"Here is fine. Take all the time you need to think about what this home has meant to you. Let me know when you are ready to move on."*

Predictable Dilemma 2:
How Can I Best Manage My Health?

Arguing with our parents about following the doctor's advice doesn't seem to work. Trying to figure out what the doctor is saying is tough enough at any age. Add to that the presence of multiple medical problems, and simply taking all prescribed medications at the right time can be a daunting task. Unless we accompany them to each appointment, it is hard to get the details we need to understand their medical issues. Concerning the question "How can I best manage my health?" older adults may simply be saying "Help me wage this war for control."

> *Their Predictable Reaction:* "I don't know what to do."
> *Our Predictable Response:* "Why are you making this so difficult?"

The HMO environment, in which many physicians practice, has made visits impersonal and communication baffling, even to those of us who are knowledgeable about medical matters. If doctors lapse into professional jargon to explain what we want to know, we feel out of control and unable to manage our health needs.

While we may understand our own reaction to jargon, we may not be prepared for the intensity of our elders' reactions to suggested medical care. Why? Because control is an entirely different issue for them than it is for us. As noted in earlier chapters, we are in the phase of life where control is assumed: We have it and use it constantly. But for our elders, control is a hot-button issue and, sadly, many would rather see their health deteriorate than give up that control. Also, deteriorating health inevitably brings up end-of-life issues they may not be ready to face.

Legacy Coach's Approach

We must intervene in our elders' attempts to manage their medical concerns.

INSIST ON CLARIFICATION

Remind the doctor that jargon makes medical conditions and treatment choices difficult to understand. "Would you explain what you just said in plain English?" "Is it possible to draw a little picture of what you are talking about?" "Do you have any basic background material we can read about this procedure?" What may seem obvious and straightforward to a medical professional may be a mystery to the layperson, particularly an elderly person whose brain, as we learned in chapter 4, may not be able to quickly process new information or new procedures, new dosages, or new ways to take a familiar treatment.

RESEARCH MORE INFORMATION ON THE ILLNESS OR TREATMENT

As legacy coaches, we must intercede and find out as much information about what the doctor said as we can. We must be profoundly tenacious and hyper-organized to fight the health-care wars. The Internet is a useful tool for researching medical subjects but can also be a source of misinformation. Stick to recognized university medical institution and government sites, such as the ones listed in this chapter's notes.

ASK FOR SUPPORT

Don't hesitate to ask the doctor or someone on his staff to recommend support or affinity groups that will explain procedures to elderly patients in a way they can understand.

By offering this kind of support when an elderly person needs it, we indicate that we understand their concerns, confusion, and need for control over their care. Most important, we signal that the elderly person is not alone on this formidable frontier.

BE YOUR LOVED ONE'S ADVOCATE

The whole issue of health care affords us an opportunity to discuss control and legacy issues. As legacy facilitators, we must demystify the jargon for our elders. ("Don't worry about the term 'edema.' It refers to that swelling you were mentioning on your kneecap." "The doctor didn't realize he lapsed into jargon. A CBC means he's going to draw a little blood, look at it under a microscope, and see if the medicine is working.") Reassure them that medicine is full of these fancy, three-dollar words and acronyms. Introduce them to the kinds of support groups that will help them deal with the health issues they face. Just as we would not want to be admitted to a hospital today without access to a patient advocate, neither should we allow our elders to operate in this world without our services as their legacy coach.

Once treatment options are clear, we can then ask our elders the kinds of questions that will give us clues about how they want to be remembered.

WHEN NEWS IS DIRE, BE PREPARED TO ACCELERATE THE AGENDA

More serious medical conditions can open a door that invites the elderly to focus on the legacy work they must do to fulfill their developmental mission. Life-threatening situations prompt them into speeding up this process. There is no doubt that once we start dealing with illness, whether it's ours or a close older friend's, all sorts of questions arise that we normally are too uncomfortable to ask. Very often there's a softening of the heart, a changed perspective on life, an enhanced opportunity to speak frankly that as legacy coaches we must facilitate.

I am reminded of the time when one of my clients fell ill, with only a matter of days to live, and I asked his wife if there was anyone who should be called. She mentioned her husband's only brother, but added that the two were estranged and hadn't spoken in a number of years. I asked her if I might notify the brother, and she said okay. I called this man, who flew halfway across the country and was at his brother's bedside the next day. I am told the two men had a meaningful and emotional exchange before my client passed away that night.

How to Say It:

The answer to the question "How can I best manage my health?" is

"Let's get more information, clarify exactly what the procedure is, talk to others who have encountered this bump in the road—and don't worry, I'll be with you every step of the way."

Predictable Dilemma 3:
How Will I Cope All by Myself?

Many of us don't encounter communication difficulties with our aging parents or clients until the person's spouse dies. Up to that time, the couple had each other to negotiate these predictable dilemmas of old age, and we may not have encountered any challenges to our ability to communicate. But once widowhood sets in, the picture changes. We realize that there has never been a more urgent need to establish and maintain rapport, yet we can hit unanticipated roadblocks. We may feel that our duty is to assume the day-to-day tasks once handled by the departed spouse at a time when the survivor resists our efforts to be helpful, yet can't seem to focus on anything but the past.

Allowing the elderly a time to grieve in the midst of devastating loss is essential. The thought uppermost in their minds is the one they may repeat again and again.

> *Their Predictable Reaction:* "I don't know where to begin."
> *Our Predictable Response:* "We need to take care of a million details."

Often we're at a loss for words to comfort a grieving parent and fear we lack empathy, in part because we are dealing with our own feelings of grief. Whatever we say seems inadequate during this difficult period. We eventually return to our agenda-packed days and may become impatient with the survivor for not getting over the death quickly and on with this business of living. We may argue with a new sense of urgency over the Predictable Dilemmas presented in this chapter and meet more resistance than we had prior to the death. We waver between sympathy and exasperation, and don't understand our parent's reluctance to acknowledge the options that these new circumstances present.

Legacy Coach's Approach

This is one communication challenge to which saying nothing may be the most appropriate response. Grief always makes us feel out of control. It is as if a raging river flips us out of the boat and sinks us, at least for a while. But at some point, grief opens a legacy door and offers an opportunity to articulate how we will honor the memory of the deceased. The responses we hear are clues to the shape of our own legacies.

I mentioned in an earlier chapter my mother's clear memory of her sister who drowned and her need to relive that day at our meeting in Starbucks. The grief she expressed some fifty years after the tragedy unexpectedly opened a legacy door that indicated how highly she values family connections, in this case a connection prematurely severed. Her vivid description of that day said two things to me: that she admires the values represented by her sister's all-too-brief life and that her own legacy—how she wants us to remember her—includes the importance she places on family ties. I will never forget that day with my mom, where I sat for three hours saying almost nothing. I didn't need to. Just giving her time and space to open up caused her to reveal more to me in that one conversation about who she is than she ever had before.

In a **family setting**, what should you do to comfort a grieving spouse or other family member?

LOOK INTENT, BUT SAY LITTLE

In fact, saying nothing would be fine, at least at first. Realize that the grief process is uneven and, to paraphrase Paul Simon's lyric in "Bridge Over Troubled Water," we need to assure the bereft person that we're sailing right behind to offer whatever support is needed. Some days our elders can talk about the deceased for hours; other days a minute's worth of conversation is unbearable to them. Some elderly mourners wish to visit the grave every day; others once a year; still others never. Recognize that everyone has a special grieving process. Whatever it is, signal that we are willing to offer support. Doing so gives seniors control over their grief. With the assurance that control is theirs, pieces of their legacy will begin to emerge.

If grief spins the elderly mourner out of control, we need to say to them first, "You are not out of control," and second, "I'm here to help you regain your sense of balance."

ASK RETROSPECTIVE QUESTIONS

A good question to ask is, "What did you want to do before you met Dad (or Mom)?" The answer may surprise us, and most certainly will be nonlinear in nature, but as we follow the twists and turns of memory, we'll be privy to the false starts and aborted plans of a life that is being recontextualized before our eyes. We must give reassurance that we are completely there, no matter where the path leads. Give elderly adults the control they need to explore, be with them for the journey, and see what emerges that can be shaped into legacy. Although new today, the dreams will be organically connected to the forces that shaped the person we know. Tell the person that those dreams can be realized in some form at the end of life. We're here to help our elder figure out what part those dreams play in the formation of that legacy.

SHARE MEMORIES OF THE DECEASED

Our own memories are important to the grieving person and can move the legacy process along. A simple reminisce—"I remember the first time Dad and I went fishing"—can start the survivor thinking in a new dimension and can be quite comforting. Be willing to share characteristics of the deceased that were admirable ("Do you remember how Dad always had a snappy comeback in uncomfortable situations that put the other person at ease?") and those that got transferred ("Every time I see my daughter persevere on a tough homework assignment, I remember Mom's determination to stick with a task, no matter how long it took to complete it.")

BE WILLING TO ARTICULATE BOTH THE PLEASANT AND THE NOT-SO-PLEASANT ASPECTS OF A LIFE

"It's too bad Uncle George was so tied up with his work. It must have been difficult for you to manage the household on your own." "I could never figure out Mom's aversion to politics, especially when such discussions meant so much to you." Statements of this kind enable the grieving person to express pent-up emotions—sorrow, pity, even anger at the deceased—and allow us to acknowledge that we understand how difficult it is to communicate negative feelings after the person is no longer here.

In a **nonfamily or professional setting,** your communication with a grieving person needs to acknowledge the deceased's contribution to life as vivid and lasting.

GET A PROFILE

By asking open-ended questions (see chapter 10), we give the mourner room to make the deceased come alive for us. Inquire about who the person was and what the mourner perceives as the deceased's contribution to family, friends, and the community at large.

Asking where a person was born might get us a one-word answer ("Chicago"), but asking where he was reared is an open-ended question that illuminates a person's entire life. Ask follow-up questions: "Raised on a ranch in Oklahoma? How did he describe that experience?" The question "How did you two meet?" invites a similar nonlinear response.

HIGHLIGHT PERCEPTIONS OF THE DECEASED PERSON'S CHARACTER

Whether we're spot on or 180 degrees off will give the grieving person a chance to agree or set the record straight. "I understand your husband worked his way through college." "Didn't your wife head several committees at your church?" Such questions assure the person that we are comfortable with these conversations and can handle anything he or she wants to discuss. What emerges is the mourner's emphasis of those parts of the deceased person's character that are most valued. "He started with fourteen dollars in his pocket and later put all his kids through school." Be willing to talk as little or as much about the person as the mourner wishes. By doing so, we signal that death is not a taboo subject for us and that we accept the mourner's feelings, whatever they are.

ACKNOWLEDGE GRIEF AS A PROFOUND STATEMENT OF LOVE

Assure the person that we are not put off by expressions of grief. I have an acquaintance, Bill, I see three times a year at professional seminars. For an entire year he failed to show and when he returned, he mentioned to me, somewhat hesitantly, that both his parents had died and his life turned upside down. "I just stopped moving," Bill explained, "I didn't come to the seminars partly because I felt like a failure for being unable to stop my tears." I explained that I saw his numbing grief as a profound statement of love and a reflection of the impact his parents' lives had on him. Then we had a long conversation about them. Afterward, when I hugged him and told him I understood what he'd been through, his relief was visible.

Assure the older person that grief may temporarily blind us or throw us off track, but that we will not be put off by it. We draw strength from grief because it proves the depth of our love. Signal that we will not avoid this subject. Even though our culture may not provide outlets for expression of grief, we understand the long process in dealing with death. Ask more questions to draw out information about the deceased.

Although many of us shy away from awkward discussions, we must realize that they provide opportunities to see a person's contribution to life as real and unique, not artificial and nonspecific.

How to Say It:

The answer to the question "How will I cope all by myself?" is

"You don't have to. I'm here to help you remember the person, draw strength from those memories, and use them to go forward with your life. Whatever your timetable, I will help you come to terms with this devastating loss."

Predictable Dilemma 4: What Should I Do about Money?

Whether the problem involves managing on a fixed income or choosing an executor and revising a will, financial and legal issues can produce tremendous conflict between the elderly person and the family, caregiver, or professional, because what's at stake are difficult issues of control and legacy. Questions regarding financial planning either open or close an important developmental door.

These emotionally charged matters can be resolved by listening to the values—expressed in almost every conversation—that are most important to the elderly person. Listening for values uncovers the raw material of organic legacy. The question "What should I do about money?" offers us a window into that person's most deeply held beliefs about himself and the world, and how he wants to be remembered.

Their Predictable Reaction: "I need to think about it."
Our Predictable Response: "But the choices seem so obvious."

From our midlife perspective, we can be stymied by an elderly person's reluctance to deal with vital money matters. Our plans make sense and can save bundles, and we feel tremendous conflict when our elders are reluctant to see it our way. Our usual response is to step up the pressure and apply arbitrary time limits that produce further delay and deflection. We try to relieve them of the financial planning burden—of setting up a monthly budget or deciding how to divide family assets—without realizing it may not be something of paramount concern to them. In fact, our focus on the subject leaves them wondering if we're more interested in *it* than in them, or if we're trying to wrest control of all they've worked for. They start to get the uneasy feeling that everyone is just waiting for the money. Moreover, they see how discussing financial issues can bring out the worst character traits in family members. We perceive unburdening them of financial concerns as a worthy goal. They react in predictable ways to our attempts to usurp the control they need to have: They hang on tight and refuse to make decisions. We become deferential and considerate; they become distant and noncommittal.

Legacy Coach's Approach

What most family members, as well as legal and financial professionals, fail to recognize is that money is the most misunderstood tool in the planning kit. The goal of most families is to avoid conflict concerning money issues; that of financial planners is to preserve a client's wealth by minimizing the tax impact on an estate and maximizing the transfer of monies to the heirs. But planners' desires to protect wealth override and undervalue its creative potential at just that time in life when creativity about money is most needed, which is when we are on the journey to discover and understand our legacy. By repositioning money as a means to an end—the end, of course, is how that person will be remembered—we can get to the issues surrounding legacy that will resonate immediately and strongly in an individual.

Remember the engineering mogul we first met in chapter 3? His advisors weren't clued in to the fact that he was struggling with legacy issues and that the plan they proposed leaving everything to his son was not going to satisfy his sense of who he was and his notion of the imprint he wanted to leave on the world. What he needed was a totally different direction—*one that he could not provide for himself*—and the financial flexibility to implement a plan that resonated with the person he perceived himself to be.

What family members need is simply to be heard.

ASK OPEN-ENDED QUESTIONS

Open-ended questions can provide clues to the person's heartfelt wishes and are a starting point in financial and legal discussions. Even if the questions are rebuffed at the time we ask them, they may resonate with the person, who will wrestle within himself for answers. While we may need to back off momentarily, we must persist in helping our elders discover the answers that will open doors to their search for a heartfelt legacy.

LISTEN FOR THE VALUES

The mogul's advisors were operating under the wrong model of planning, one that focuses 98 percent on preserving wealth and only 2 percent on creating something else. What they needed to do was reverse that formula and see the money for its broader potential. Money is a tool, not an end in itself, to offer opportunities for a person's legacy to mean something outside of himself and his family. Money needs to be used to reflect the values a person wants to pass on to future generations. The trick is to discover what those values are. That's where our communication skills as legacy coach come into the picture.

RETHINK THE MODEL

Why didn't the mogul's family seem to him a fitting legacy? Why wasn't the mogul able to determine for himself how he wanted to be remembered? In my experience, wealth is a destabilizing force in a person's life. Many successful retired men (and it is still mostly men who fall into this category; it will be interesting to see how successful corporate women fare as they begin to retire in the next ten years) believe that the only reason anyone cares about them is because they have money. These guys belong to the Emotionally Unavailable Club. They focused so intently on work their entire adult lives that they failed to bond with their families and contribute to their communities. Regardless of their public personas, they are bitter below the surface. They feel they don't owe their families anything, because they have already given them everything, not realizing that material possessions are no substitute for emotional connection, for simply being available.

ASSESS CAREER IMPACT

How do they develop this attitude? I think it is because they get bad advice as they rise the corporate ladder, which is, "You're on your own, bucko, and we are keeping score. You are the sum of the decisions you make and the amount you add to the pot." Translation? The male group dynamic dictates that men equate performance with worth. If we are what we accomplish, then many men at life review feel they come up short. In the constant drive to earn the highest score, they have painful regrets and a sense of isolation. When they reach old age they realize that money turned out not to be *it*. And if money is not *it*, then they *don't* want to be remembered by how much money they made. But how they *do* want to be remembered is hidden from their view. In the majority of cases, they are unable to find answers on their own.

CONSIDER FAMILY HISTORY

Another powerful legacy-coach tool is to look back into the elder person's family history for answers to certain financial and legal questions. How did Grandpa solve this particular issue? What was it about the way he chose to be remembered that pleased members of the family, or displeased them? Do we want to go that route again or create a different path?

BE CREATIVE, FLEXIBLE, AND PATIENT

One doesn't need to be a corporate mogul to feel this desire to be remembered for the life that we have led. But life is confusing and more so the longer we live. By asking open-ended questions, we can help our elders grapple with the life review process, with its promise of open-ended possibilities and the flexibility to make things happen. Some senior adults struggle with a finished product, be it an established trust, a completely executed will, or a monthly budget. They need our creativity to gain a different perspective on their lives. They need our flexibility to help them maneuver the uneven paths of life review. They need our patience to let themes and reconsiderations take hold and settle in. They need to know they can create a new meaning or ending to their journey at any time. In fact, I often counsel planners to use the words "create," "generate," "establish," and "innovate" as often as possible with their clients.

In a family setting, our elders need the same kind of language that indicates creative ideas about forming a legacy are always appreciated.

How to Say It:

To the question "What should I do about money?" we might respond

"Take all the time you need to arrive at the answer that best reflects you and the life you've lived."

Predictable Dilemma 5:
What Is the Right Way to Say Good-bye?

When the end is near, legacy starts to emerge with more clarity and urgency, but we have to listen carefully for repeated words, phrases, and ideas to distill the values by which the person wants to be remembered. To the question, "What is the right way to say good-bye?" many elderly people may either be uncomfortable or at a loss to explain their feelings.

Their Predictable Reaction: "Where did the time go?"
Our Predictable Response: "Don't worry, everything will be okay."

Contemplating final wishes is sometimes more than we can bear, because we don't want to face life without the person. We avoid bringing up the subject, because it makes *us* uncomfortable. If our elders bring it up, we try to minimize its magnitude. "You are going to live forever." "Let's not get all dark and gloomy."

Legacy Coach's Approach

Part of saying the right good-bye is giving the person control over the form that good-bye will take. After control is no longer an issue, we can help the elderly manage this predictable dilemma. Through our efforts they sense a kindred spirit and begin to trust that the departure legacy they have in mind will work and be meaningful.

It is important that none of us leaves this world mute. Our wishes must be known and they must make sense to family members and circumstances. In order to facilitate the elderly person in this all-important mission, we might raise some of the questions below:

WHO NEEDS THE MOST HEALING?

Sometimes one child or survivor of the elderly person is a lost soul, disconnected from family and other relationships. Encourage the elderly person to address some specific comments to that person. Such an effort will be remembered and may start the process of healing a wrenched heart.

WHO NEEDS THE MOST COMFORT?

Sometimes the strongest survivor is the one who will be most affected by the elderly person's death. Does that person need some special support from the elderly person before that moment comes?

WHO NEEDS A WAKE-UP CALL?

Help the elderly person find words of advice or wisdom for the survivors who may be wasting precious time, not fulfilling their potential, or making trouble for those who care about them.

WHO NEEDS SPECIAL PROTECTION?

I think of a friend's special-needs sister, who will not be able to live independently. Does the elderly person want to ensure the sister's perpetual care? What words can the elderly person impart to an individual who has limited understanding of life's end?

WHO NEEDS A NEW START?

Is there someone in the family whose life is derailed, but who, with some extra attention, could learn to succeed?

Asking these kinds of questions can facilitate the right way to say goodbye. Helping the elderly person find appropriate answers to these questions returns a sense of control at this crucial stage. Facilitating the responses helps the elderly person's legacy to emerge.

DELIVER SUPPORT THROUGH ANY MEANS AVAILABLE

Support can be delivered in person, by audio or video tape, or through creation of a special program. The right way to say good-bye is not predicated on planning and prefunding the funeral. It is based on ensuring that the elderly person has enough control over predictable encounters to address end-of-life concerns. As legacy coaches, we also derive comfort by asking these final questions and wisdom from helping to form the answers.

How to Say It:

The answer to the question "What is the right way to say good-bye?" involves an attempt to mine the deepest levels of a person's legacy. At life's end, the meaningful answers we seek are prompted by profound questions legacy coaches find the courage to ask:

> *"Mom, is there anyone else we need to reach? Is there anything more you want to say? Are we both clear about the way you want to be remembered?"*

The Redemptive Power of Relationships

Sometimes I become aware of elderly people who never found a legacy coach to help them unlock the meaning of their lives. What was special about those lives will remain undiscovered forever. Perhaps they were angry, bitter individuals who alienated themselves from the very people they supported for decades. Left in old age to manage themselves, they probably continued to control their environment while the other, more lasting piece of the developmental pie never got touched.

Since every life affects many people in many ways, it is essential for us to master the communication skills that can pierce through senior adults' control armor and get to their core. Only through our relationship with this older generation can we learn which communication skills discussed in this chapter and throughout the book will be effective and which might fail. Our relationship with the elderly has the power to cut through the various experiences and get to the heart of their matter. Using our best control-protection strategies and most creative coaching skills, we often sense a legacy emerging that provides us with rewards we never knew existed. This is a legacy that begins to shape who *we* are, one we may someday want to pass on to others. The best legacy coaches offer the profound power of relationship to those elderly people they know, either personally or professionally, and discover that both parties are redeemed by the experience.

The world can be a dark and hostile place to our elderly. As physical strength ebbs, they can become prisoners of their psyches and withdraw deep into themselves. It's clear that control is a dominant and pervasive developmental need, but while old age demands control, it does not necessarily offer the elderly the ability to manage end-of-life tasks alone. Most of the depression we see in old people results from too little connection with an understanding, caring person. Left to fend for themselves (difficult for anyone under the best of circumstances), without anyone to ask the right questions and give the right support, our elders don't accomplish their legacy mandate. Our relationship with them is powerful stuff that redeems both generations and can mean the difference between a life that falls muted by the wayside and one that is remembered and cherished.

PART THREE

NEW STRATEGIES FOR COMMUNICATING WITH OLDER ADULTS

———

This section outlines practical strategies we can use to facilitate communication with senior adults. Such strategies can create opportunities for engaging in dialogues and forging meaningful connections. Learning to listen for significant thought patterns and understanding the substance, not merely the facts, of their conversations is key. Additional anecdotes reveal the importance of signaling verbally and nonverbally that we appreciate the values seniors express in their conversations and want to help them discover what role those values play in forming their legacies.

SEVEN

Why Is This So Hard?

EXPECTATIONS, PROGRESS, AND SETBACKS IN BUILDING
BETTER RELATIONSHIPS WITH OLDER ADULTS

"We see things not as they are, but as we are."

—*H. M. Tomlinson*

WE are now acquainted with the developmental drivers that motivate older people and the issues underlying the unique ways they express themselves. We've learned how to listen with the ear of a legacy coach. We feel committed to this new role and inspired to make it work in ways that benefit members of the older, younger, and our own generations.

We may have enjoyed some resounding initial successes. Suddenly our elders are responsive, communicating, and reveling in the attention we've focused on them. They blossom, as we expect they would. We feel energized in our coaching mode.

Then perhaps we hit a snag, a bump in the road in our communication with the elderly person. We ask an open-ended question and get stonewalled or bullied with a response like, "Why are you asking me that? That is none of your business." We hear a new detail in a repeated story that intrigues us and seek more information, only to get a shrug and a yawn. We try the plant-and-wait technique—and find we're still waiting for answers to important matters several weeks, even months after we first asked. Our developmental agenda demands we get the ball rolling, sew things up, and complete the task, so we begin to doubt our newfound abilities as legacy coaches; we may even start to doubt the wisdom of such an approach. What do we do when these new techniques don't work, our patience runs thin, or time is short?

The Cold Reality of a Biased Perspective

As we begin our work with senior adults, we have to appreciate that no matter how excited we are about this new role, both parties are filled with collective biases that can influence the success of our interactions. We can't pretend we're working with clean slates and that everyone will respond to our coaching techniques in the same way every time we use them. Our initial successes may, in fact, backfire, with our elderly acquaintances becoming more entrenched in counterproductive habits, less willing to make a decision, less responsive, or angrier than they were before we intervened.

If we get this sort of response, we must step back and realize that we're dealing with people who have lived long and complex lives, and that these long-lived, complex individuals may be full of life experiences and chronic conflicts that are outside of their developmental issues. These conflicts might relate to secret oaths of prior days; things that happened they swore they would never forgive, forget, or reveal; hurts that they are unable to dismiss. The conflicts are part of who they are. We can't assume that the developmental agenda is the only pressure they are responding to.

Consider alcoholics. We might think that when they get sober, all will be fine and a wonderful person will emerge. But that's not always true. What we discover, in some cases, are extremely unhappy people who were sedating themselves with alcohol and are still the same miserable, not very pleasant people who may become addicted to other substances.

Think about elderly people who had unhappy marriages. Even though they are responding to developmental drivers pushing them toward acceptance of their lives, such insight doesn't make up for the fact that their marriage didn't work out and may have left a lot of scars. In these cases, older adults are operating under the influence of two dominant emotions—fear and anger—well illustrated in the movie *About Schmidt,* where the recently retired sixty-seven-year-old Schmidt loses his wife suddenly and slowly becomes aware of how dependent he was on her and how empty his life is now. He tries to engage his daughter in the caretaker role once occupied by his wife, but the daughter has other ideas, which include marrying and getting as far away from her emotionally distant father as she can.

We have to realize that our appreciation of the developmental agendas driving older adults doesn't mitigate those lifelong pressing issues that may rise to the surface in unexpected and, for us, unpleasant ways. These long lives are not bound by our assumptions and cannot be reduced to simple theories. It is important that we not be discouraged or, worse yet, defeated if our new strategies don't always work.

The Parent Trap

When we begin our work with older adults, we need to be aware of the risk of reliving what I call the Parent Trap. The Parent Trap is a reminder that, as we raised our kids, we could not take their developmental surges personally. We needed to see a two-year-old's tantrums or a teenager's aloofness in the context of overall developmental growth and not as a personal affront. The more we manage our expectations about certain developmentally induced behaviors, the more successful we'll feel as parents—and as legacy coaches.

As *About Schmidt* suggests, there are rarely any neat endings to life. Just as many of us were ambivalent about our parenting role—after all, there was a lot of good stuff and some really bad stuff most of us had to deal with—we must realize that legacy coaching demands a similar kind of commitment to the well-being of another individual. As parents, we didn't back down from the challenges of raising our kids. As legacy coaches, we must commit to the effort it takes to establish and maintain good connections with our elders.

Not every communication technique we read about will work. Sometimes the technique will work and sometimes it won't. One of my colleagues, Arthur, spent hours researching, selecting, and then buying a vacation package he thought both he and his recently widowed father would enjoy. His father seemed agreeable, only to call him a week before departure date to tell him he was backing out. Exasperated, Arthur hung up the phone without even asking why. A few days later, Arthur's dad called back to suggest an entirely different kind of vacation. Arthur chose to ignore his dad's "erratic" behavior and began to look at the signals he may have missed in their communication about taking a vacation together.

Arthur had always had a stormy relationship with this parent; they were usually at odds over many things. He admitted to me that his father never seemed to take the advice he offered and to this day he is distressed over his dad's lack of urgency, repetitiveness, focus on details, and profound ingratitude on matters more weighty than where to spend leisure time. He once took these traits about his dad as a personal affront for all the effort he makes on his behalf. Dad "keeps him at arm's length" and "changes directions" in his thinking without informing him that Plan A was not to his liking. Arthur now sees this behavior as his father's way of maintaining control and resisting intrusions into his life.

What's the message Arthur might have taken away from his dad's abrupt change of plans? There's a wide range of what we call normal in people, and what Arthur perceived as normal—that where they vacationed was less important than simply being together at the agreed-upon time—was not Dad's vision of what was right for him. Perhaps Arthur didn't pay enough attention to earlier signals or ask the right questions; perhaps he did, but Dad truly did change his mind and didn't realize the repercussions of doing so. To his credit, Arthur never made his father feel bad about the lost deposit or the scheduling chaos he had to sort out; he accepted the situation and vowed to himself to respect his father's wishes—and listen more attentively in future exchanges.

Sustaining the Commitment

We need to understand that unpredictability is part of life. Part of our commitment to legacy coaching requires that we become adept at adjusting the sails or we'll be cursing the weather every day. A secret storm could be brewing at any time and we must be prepared to face what comes.

How seriously we take our decision to become legacy coaches is a predictor of the results we achieve. We won't be able to sustain our commitment if we are blown out of the water every time we get shot down or scolded. How do we sustain our momentum?

Many of us who work with older clients or interact with elderly relatives have this dilemma: We want to give them a meaningful gift, something they will like. But they have everything they need and end up unhappy or returning whatever we buy. I thought a friend of mine came up with the perfect solution to buying Christmas gifts for his mother. Since she was very difficult to please and returns were inevitable, he decided to take her to a major department store and let her pick out whatever she wanted. He flew to her city, took her to a store, and, after much fussing and trying on and discussion with a very patient salesperson, she made her selections. Accompanying her to the cash register, he described to me his feelings of satisfaction as he surrendered his credit card and gave her a wink and a knowing look that said, "Well, isn't this wonderful? Aren't I clever to have thought of this solution and aren't you pleased?" This mood vanished when she caught his eye and his mood and said, "You should have thought of this sooner!" *Bam!* Talk about a shot to the gut. . . .

The point is we must realize that occasionally we'll get blasted for our best efforts. Committing to the job of legacy coach is 90 percent of the battle and promotes the discipline that causes us to stick with it, through thick and thin. We are not going to resolve every issue for our parents or older colleagues, but what we can do is create an opportunity that will allow clarification and repair to happen. Our parents and other members of their generation created opportunities for us to grow in every way; we in turn must do the same for them.

A legacy coach's goal is to encourage older adults to successfully navigate the challenges of aging. Some things will surface; some won't. We cannot presume to be psychotherapists. All we can do is offer the best possible environment for communication and reflection, and hope the elderly person responds and gets done whatever he or she needs to do. We can facilitate developmental issues by seeing control as a major war and intervening whenever possible, by asking open-ended questions and acting on the responses we hear. We can't make every life perfect; some seniors we know will die grumpy, with their legacies unrealized, carrying their anger and fear to the grave. Our job is to make it possible for the most healing, insight, and spiritual progress to take place.

Self-management—the idea that people can run their lives without any connections—doesn't usually work and leaves people lonely and afraid. A person leading such a life has no ability to read both the condition of the boat and the weather at the same time. It's just impossible; we need both pieces of information accurately and often throughout life. Egocentricity and disconnect are painful, but there are many examples of people, like Schmidt, who have withdrawn into their bitterness and don't absorb any outside influences until very late in life, if they ever do.

As was illustrated in the last chapter, there are many things in life that we cannot obtain on our own. Part of the legacy coach's job is to be sensitive to those times when asking the right question with the right inflection, waiting an extra second or two to hear an answer, or pausing a conversation at just the right moment, gives the elderly person an opportunity to see another possibility, to recontextualize an experience and glean an insight that might never have been reached without our facilitation. Legacy coaching enables us to understand the effectiveness of this approach and gives us the tools to use it.

Another goal is to rise above the setbacks and see our legacy-coaching role as a grand expression of the Serenity Prayer, in that we must have courage to move into places where we can do some good, accept situations over which we have no control, and be empowered with the wisdom to know the difference. The developmental model helps us figure out that difference.

This kind of facilitation is a realistic goal, not pie-in-the-sky at all. Yes, it's a big job and to think otherwise is to set ourselves up for disappointment.

Changing the Model

Understanding developmental conflicts of old age is one thing; using communication techniques in live settings is something else. Be aware that, according to behavioral psychologists such as B. F. Skinner, a behavior we are trying to extinguish may actually intensify in response to initial intervention. That is, the behavior, attitude, or assumption we are trying to change can actually get worse before it gets better, if it improves at all. Our first efforts at communication, rather than providing the soothing interaction we anticipated, may prove provocative.

How should we respond if our efforts blow up in our face?

1. *Back off and reexamine.* We need to view our efforts as objectively as possible. Did we present the idea in a rushed way? Did we withhold key information that might be relevant?

2. *Return to a more neutral position* than we initially took, or drop the subject entirely. Realize that the elderly person may have been in a different mental orbit and not ready to absorb new information.

3. *Don't take a negative reaction personally.* We may need to figure out an alternate strategy to get our point across.

4. *Redraft the plan.* Don't try to rehammer the same points that backfired the first time around. If we get locked out of our house, what would we do? Standing at the front door hoping our keys will appear won't work. We might try alternative entry points: a window or the back door. We may call a neighbor for help or support. In the same manner, if a communication issue is important enough, we need to reframe it in different language or at a less hectic pace than we originally did. If the elderly person still isn't receptive, drop it.

5. *Keep our goal in mind.* Were certain words, topics, or assumptions more provocative than we'd anticipated? Select other options and see if they get a better reaction.

6. *Look at the timing.* Were *we* in a bad mental or physical place when the subject was mentioned? Try a different venue or another time and see if the response is better. In many instances we try to get something accomplished and don't realize the setting is just not appropriate. For example, bringing up medication issues at a family celebration might seem to us to be a supportive way to do it, but might draw fire rather than appreciation from the elderly person to whom the comments are directed.

7. *Be sure to prepare for the encounter.* Doing our homework allows us to create a nonlinear environment in which a conversation can work. Presenting unpleasant or undesirable choices in the heat of battle or in the midst of a life-changing decision is often counterproductive.

Setbacks in a Professional Venue

In a professional setting, it may be more difficult to avoid setbacks and repair any miscommunications that may arise. Remember the mogul whose advisors were at a loss to know how to repair the damage that was done in the meeting where they missed the mark and he stormed out? The problem was not lack of preparation, but misjudging the amount and type of persuasion that would work best with this individual.

Professionals have two communication limitations.

1. *They have a defined goal,* and need to meet preset objectives.

2. *They usually have time restrictions,* which limit their opportunity for the kinds of open-ended, nonlinear conversations that can reveal the insights that may be relevant to the task at hand.

In a family setting, we can structure time and conversations to accommodate the elderly person's pace and mood. There are other limitations to the family setting, having to do with personal involvement that distorts objectivity, but we can usually create an environment that gives an elderly person time to respond to our suggestions.

In a professional setting, the agenda is set before the elderly person even walks in the door. Sometimes that agenda misses the mark and produces no progress toward the goal.

Dealing with the elderly in a professional setting is a subject worthy of an entire book, and we'll discuss effective communication strategies in more detail in Appendix I. The point of this section's discussion is to reframe setbacks in professional settings as opportunities. By understanding what went wrong and why, we can increase contact and refine goals. Setbacks allow us to adjust our expectations of what is possible in any situation. They are not only instructive but also give us a greater arena in which to practice the skills we need to become effective with seniors. Our usefulness is predicated on how well we can tolerate these setbacks and use our skills in trying to reestablish the connection.

In the case of the aforementioned mogul, the professional who best knew the family contacted the mogul's wife for clues to where his planning group may have gone astray. This professional did not take the initial rebuff as a signal to quit. He persevered, confident that he would be able to present a more attractive alternative after gathering more information.

To reestablish the connection with older clients and patients, try the following techniques:

1. *Breathe and refocus.* Did we expect to hit a home run the first time at bat? If we did, was that a reasonable expectation?

2. *Try a different approach,* perhaps interviewing a family member or colleague.

3. *Rethink the goal.* Is the elderly person capable of understanding and agreeing to a radical new plan? Can the plan be modified or described in different language that might resonate with the client?

4. *Redefine progress.* Although our midlife agendas demand we cross off as many items as possible at day's end, progress with the elderly takes the courage to know that we tried something, whether it worked or not, and that we're committed to reengagement that can bring us closer to the goal.

Breakthroughs and Setbacks

As with any personal relationship, ours with our senior friends, colleagues, and relatives can be fraught with the typical highs and lows of daily living. Sometimes our efforts to connect will be rewarded, sometimes we'll be rebuffed. As legacy coaches, we need to create a supportive environment for every senior we know. The payoff for us is tremendous: The longer they live, the more time we have to facilitate the discovery of their legacy and benefit from its wisdom and insights. If we communicate easily and well, this process is not a chore, but a blessing.

EIGHT

Figuring Out
the Right Signals

HIDDEN COMMUNICATION CHALLENGES
IN EVERYDAY LIVING

"Listen or thy tongue will keep thee deaf."

—*Native American Proverb*

THERE are as many nonverbal as there are verbal indicators that predict the success of our conversations with senior adults. While communication between any two people contains seen and unseen, spoken and unspoken challenges, communication between the generations is particularly sensitive to such factors as timing, pauses, tone of voice—even the way we phrase our questions—because we may bump up against developmental issues that trigger strong responses and create distance rather than connection. This chapter looks at the hidden verbal and nonverbal signals that can affect communication with our elders.

Our communication goal may be simple: to persuade Mom to spend the holidays with us. Or it may be more complex: to ask Dad how he found the strength to succeed after a painful career setback. We sense that how we phrase the question, even the moment we choose to ask it, could significantly alter the direction and dimension of the discussion. Below are specific strategies by which we can gauge the elderly person's receptivity to any topic and enhance our ability to discuss it without judging that person's competence. These strategies are de-signed to create a dialogue that immediately offers control to seniors, which is a key to connecting with this age group. With control no longer an issue, we create the space for legacy issues to surface.

The Dangling Conversation: The Importance of Settling Rituals

"I was never the same after Myrtle died, you know. . . ."

In the conversation at Starbucks, my mom took about twenty minutes to settle in and gauge my demeanor (relaxed, focused on her instead of my elec-tronic gadgets or departure schedule), before she began a vividly detailed story about an incident in her life that profoundly affected her: the death of her beloved older sister when she was a child. I knew about this family tragedy, but had never heard her describe it with the intensity and focus she did that af-ternoon. I've often thought about what I did and did not do that allowed these memories to surface. The answers I found, outlined below, can improve any communication with senior adults.

Settling In

What was it about our interaction at Starbucks that caused my mother to re-veal such vivid details? As noted in chapter 5, I had three hours to spend with her before my departure for the airport, so instead of the harried, hurried, preoccupied middle-aged executive who usually greeted her, she saw across the table a relaxed, attentive son who focused only on her. Even so, she took twenty minutes to begin her story. During that time I purposely hadn't said much—I wanted to let her talk that day. But I realize I opened a communica-tions door by giving her ample time to express what I now call her "settling rituals."

Many of us have experienced the nonverbal sensation of "picking up right where we left off" in our daily conversations with friends, colleagues, and rel-atives. Even if we haven't seen a person in months or years, we sometimes experience an instant "click" that allows us to get to the heart of a conversation quickly.

On the other hand, we can experience a delay or some difficulty in getting to the substance or purpose of a discussion, particularly if we don't know the other person well or a long agenda is anticipated and we need to gauge how receptive the other person is to the topic we want to raise. That's why large meetings usually begin with some sort of introductory comments before the keynote speaker begins: to give audience members time to settle down, get out note-taking implements, stop rustling papers, turn off cell phones and pagers, take a last sip of coffee, and then focus on the matter to be presented.

In my experience interviewing elderly clients and talking with older members of my family throughout the years, I've noted that senior adults rarely experience a quick "click" that can jump-start a conversation. Whether they have some physical problem, such as poor eyesight or hearing loss, or they've been conditioned to feel marginalized and defensive at the outset by our obliviousness to their control needs, senior adults engage in what I term "settling rituals" before they are ready to discuss what's really on their minds, or before they're comfortable enough to hear what we have to say.

Their settling rituals involve getting physically comfortable in their chairs (a longer process for them than for us), engaging in nonlinear discussions before revealing more heartfelt material, and gauging how receptive we are to them. One of my colleagues, who saw an elderly woman a couple of times a week in his medical rounds at a nursing home, noted that she loved to knit. When he began bringing her small balls of yarn, she began looking forward to their interviews, rather than resisting his intrusion into her day. By adapting to her settling rituals, he noted she was able to focus more quickly, which made the time he spent with her more productive.

After twenty minutes of nonlinear conversation with my mother that day in Starbucks, I felt that "click" and attempted to refocus the discussion. "Mom," I asked, "have you heard from anyone in the family lately?" Then I remained silent.

This gentle probe unleashed a flood of memories. My relaxed demeanor signaled that I was in a frame of mind where I could listen attentively to what she had to say about a topic her internal agenda was compelling her to review.

What followed was an intense monologue that held clues to my mother's values and how she wants to be remembered. We'll learn to listen for and respond to the values contained in any discussion in chapter 10. Our goal here is to figure out the initial steps we need to take to get that conversation going.

The factors that made this Starbucks conversation a success contained important rules and tools about nonverbal cues for improving our ability to listen and respond to older adults.

Timing Rules

Start with the right attitude. The potential for meaningful dialogue is lurking beneath the surface of every conversation with a senior adult. Assume this potential exists, but don't force it. No one ever forced a meaningful conversation. Every discussion serves as a building block toward some goal, even if its purpose or objective isn't clear, so resist the urge to achieve resolution or a satisfying conclusion quickly.

Read the start-up code by learning to decipher an older person's settling rituals. Identify the components of the ritual, which include conversation topics and the amount of time devoted to settling into the discussion. Resist the urge to shorten the ritual. It only produces anxiety and mistrust. If asked, reciprocate with sincerity and adequate details about the topic the senior adult has chosen. Summing up the entire family's situation or health as "fine" is insincere and ineffective.

Learn to accept the topics. Determine what topics are comfortable for the person we are seeing or interviewing. If we start with general topics like the weather, health, family, and sports, we'll learn which ones lead to the person's heart and spark the desire to reflect and communicate.

Don't try to predict when the developmental alarm bell is going to ring. Meaningful moments are not always based on cause and effect. They can appear in an otherwise mundane discussion. Be prepared to shift gears quickly, but be aware that we can undo months of progress by getting too aggressive when seniors give us a "time-to-act" signal. Remember who has earned and needs the control in the interaction.

We need to keep track of our findings. The more personal our recall at the next meeting, the better the communication we'll have going forward.

Watch for a change in subject. Don't be surprised by quick transitions out of and into substantive discussion. The space between the warm-up and a serious conversation can be one nonlinear phrase.

Wait for the conversation to end naturally. In conversation with parents or older clients, how many of us have been guilty of answering a question before it's been asked? Of solving a problem before the older person mentions it? The person we're talking with isn't halfway through their explanation and we're already cross-examining or firing off solutions. We're treating the condition before the patient has finished presenting the symptoms. Baby boomers in particular must realize that settling rituals must be observed and cannot be rushed in our interactions with senior adults.

How to Say It:

Our developmental agendas demand that items get done every day; therefore, we often look for the condensed version of wherever the conversation seems to be headed. Effective communication with the elderly is impossible if we are determined to stick to our agendas. We need to let our agendas go and observe theirs.

> **Doctor to senior adult patient:** *"Forgive me, Mrs. Jones, I realize this routine procedure is not routine to you. Let me explain it in more detail."*

> **Son to elderly parents:** *"I guess I jumped the gun. If you need more time, take it. Do you have questions I could answer?"*

> **Financial planner to client:** *"There's absolutely no rush to set up this account. Why don't you think about it and let me know if shifting these funds makes sense to you."*

Leave with the right attitude. Departure rituals are settling rituals in reverse and require equal attention. As with most conversations, ours with senior adults are effective when we take the time to sum up and determine a plan of future action. With seniors we need to clarify and reinforce mutual values, then decide when to talk again.

How to Say It:

"I've enjoyed our talk, Mrs. Jones. I agree there's no need to rush this procedure. You let me know when we need to meet again."

WITH practice, we can become proficient at identifying settling rituals. Observing them will greatly enhance our conversations with elderly people. Why? Because these rituals help older adults gauge how available and open we are to true communication about subjects that are meaningful to them.

A Word about Setting

The setting in which we attempt to converse is crucial because not all environments are conducive to meaningful discussion. Some settings can signal thoughtfulness; some can signal a timed event (can we relax and settle in, or do we need to get back in an hour?). Forgetting to disconnect our electronic leashes can undermine an effective setting as can obsessing about the food, service, lighting, or noise. The most ineffective settings include doctors' offices and noisy restaurants. Avoid them for important conversations. Doctors' offices usually have a sterile smell and harsh lighting, and a sense that we lack control over our lives. Noisy restaurants are distracting and impersonal places where it's hard to focus and hear clearly.

Some of the most effective and productive settings for conversations are out of doors.

The Garden

Outside settings can be effective for promoting conversation with older adults because for many of us our happiest memories are of events that have taken place outdoors. It doesn't matter how we get outside and it doesn't matter how long we stay. What matters is that we experience fresh air and allow it to evoke memories. The outside world brings to the forefront a different part of our essence, particularly in senior adults with limited mobility.

The Walk

Face-to-face is not always the best way to spark conversation. Some discussions are best approached from the side, not head on. Some topics don't arise unless they are approached obliquely. A walk provides a kind of safety shield, another focus in an interesting venue, especially when the topics are difficult. Don't discount the warm-up or settling in phase of the discussion during your walk. Be open to any subject that arises.

I spent a few days with a client when she was undergoing treatment at a clinic to learn how to manage her diabetes. We had several interactions having to do with her health, but the best conversations we had were on our walks between her residence hall and the building where she ate her meals. She was a very bright seventy-eight-year-old widow, and at the end of her stay understood the reasons why she needed to change her lifestyle and eating habits. About twenty minutes into one of our walks, our focus shifted from the business at hand to more personal matters, and we've been friends ever since. A couple of years after I represented her, she called me at my office one day and said, "I hope I'm not imposing on your time, but I need to talk with you. My children are very upset with me."

"What seems to be the problem?" I asked.

"I have a boyfriend."

She probably would never have felt comfortable phoning me with that information had we not taken those walks that enabled more personal information to be exchanged.

The Drive

A drive is like a walk on wheels. When we are having trouble resolving an important issue, getting in the car and going somewhere or nowhere at all can take the conversation in a new direction. As with a walk, this exchange does not have to be face-to-face and might make the older person more comfortable testing out an idea or a theory about something personal or revelatory. We want to expose the older person to new external stimuli and see what bubbles to the surface. Sometimes the open air and skies inspire insights and ideas, and relax inhibitions. For example, an old tree coming into view might inspire a boyhood tale and take life review in a different direction.

By creating another environment for memories to be stimulated, sorted, and discussed, we open the door to the world of legacy formation. Any such opportunity to inspire creative thinking reaps vast rewards.

The Visit

Particularly if the elderly person has limited mobility, going to visit someone provides a focus outside their usual venue for new ideas to arise in the conversation. Seeing a newborn member of the family can bring up associations with other family members. ("I don't believe it. This baby looks exactly like your Uncle George when he was born!" "Isn't it amazing that this tiny thing has my mother's eyes?") Follow up with good questions. ("What else can you remember that was distinctive about Grandma?") Listening with our legacy-coach ears shows genuine interest in the answers.

Signaling Tools

Signaling tools—techniques that can be used to indicate we're aware of the developmental issues our seniors face and are available to discuss them—come in two forms: *nonverbal,* in the form of body language and pauses; and *verbal,* in the way we phrase questions. Using communication radar, a form of intuition most of us possess, we can become alert to moments that are ripe for intimate connection. In senior adults, communication radar is highly tuned to the signals we send indicating an attempt to tamper with their control or legacy issues without their permission. Our goal is to signal back that we are developmentally friendly. Like all essential skills in life, we need to practice these signals in order to perfect them.

Nonverbal Signals

Body Language

The most important communication tool we have may be nonverbal, that is, what we convey without words. It has been reported that the human body can produce more than seven hundred thousand unique movements that combine to create nonverbal communication. **These nonverbal cues convey the whole story about the real meaning behind what we say.** They either validate or undermine our words. It is important to be aware of the cues we are giving and the ones we are getting in return from older adults.

As a result of my years of experience interviewing older people, I have learned to signal nonverbally that nothing is more important than our conversation. To do that, I focus completely on the person with whom I'm conversing. Here are important nonverbal cues that indicate our receptivity to the senior's message:

Sit in a relaxed manner and face the other person. This body positioning indicates to the elderly person that we're focused and intent on what they've got to say. While side-by-side discussions serve the purpose of changing or deepening the content, or allowing difficult topics to be expressed, facing a person indicates the topic he or she has chosen is of interest and we're prepared to discuss it.

Make friendly eye contact. Avoid the intense, oppressive stare that makes a listener uncomfortable. Elderly people might misread such intensity as a desire to control the conversation. The message we want to send is that we are tracking, not driving, what the person is saying.

Keep your hands folded in your lap. Crossing our arms in front of us indicates a lack of openness to the older person, as if we have already drawn conclusions about what they are saying. Hands placed loosely in our laps indicate the ease and openness we want to project.

Relax the shoulders. We tend to carry too much tension in our shoulders. Hunched-up shoulders indicate tightness and imply lack of availability that can dampen our attempts at meaningful conversation.

Breathe deeply. Taking deeper breaths slows the pace and calms both parties to a conversation.

*   *   *

THESE nonverbal cues are also a good checklist for reading what the older person's body language is signaling us.

Is the person ready to listen to what we have to say? How relaxed is this person? Check breathing rate. Is he or she making eye contact or distracted? How do we read the body language? Are arms crossed in front, signaling closure, or relaxed and held at the sides, indicating openness?

Does the conversation seem to unsettle the person? Look for nonverbal cues of nervousness as conversation topics shift. For example, clearing the throat, fiddling with hair or beard, pulling at skin, or wringing hands could indicate heartfelt material is being processed but is not yet fully understood.

Pauses

Once the conversation begins, let it flow. Don't try to fill in the voids. The San Francisco matron whom we met in chapter 5 spoke with me for hours while her bevy of assistants, hired to keep her on a tight schedule, checked to make sure she was all right. More than one hour into our conversation, she stopped talking. I remained silent but attentive, and she then uttered that nonlinear statement about doctors not knowing everything. She didn't explain her statement at first and I didn't follow up, knowing that because she spoke with such emotion, the subject would come up again. Her pause and then her outburst signaled to me that she was eager to explore a topic she hadn't spoken about in forty years: her special-needs child. Waiting another minute or two—observing her pause so that she could gather her thoughts—proved to be the key communication technique in that long conversation. That silent beat allowed her to open up about a difficult subject and led, ultimately, to the discovery of her organic legacy.

The woman we first met in chapter 3, whose father died the night after his wife was found asphyxiated in their bathroom, was angry with her dad for years. But in that conversation with me, she was able to reexamine this incident and forgive him for ignoring doctors' orders that left her and her sister orphaned at a young age. I said nothing in response to her initial statement,

"I haven't thought about this in thirty years." I merely listened intently to the nonlinear thoughts as she began to reformulate them into a significant insight.

Here are some important points to remember when using pauses:

Silence is not toxic. Pauses in any conversation serve a purpose, but with senior adults they allow the unconscious to reconfigure itself and catch up with the conscious. When that happens, those all-important nonlinear thoughts start to emerge.

Don't predict the path. Once we begin to hear nonlinear thoughts, we can assist the pathfinder but not determine the path. If we remain silent but interested and focused, nonlinear thoughts will organize themselves and perhaps emerge as an epiphany that can lead to legacy.

Be prepared for the unexpected surfacing of a major life theme. "Doctors don't know everything." "My life was never the same after Myrtle died." "I haven't thought about this in thirty years." These are examples of nonlinear comments that emerged after pauses in conversations I had with older individuals and foreshadowed something greater than the words they uttered. Once the insight or incident emerges, senior adults can then begin to decipher meaning and assign a legacy weight to it.

Silence is sometimes the best response to emerging life themes. When these nonlinear statements start to emerge, sometimes the best approach is to pause and say nothing, but indicate with our body language that we're "all ears" and eager to hear more. Let the person breathe and don't try to anticipate what he or she will say next.

How to Say It:

In response to senior adults' pauses, say nothing, but look attentive! Pauses in a senior adult's conversation may indicate the person is wrestling with a moment from the past that changed the course of a life. What follows after this pause may be a statement that is crucial to our understanding of who that person is. Further discussion may begin to reveal or clarify a legacy.

When our communication radar senses that a nonlinear moment will pass unless we offer some sort of reinforcement, we need to respond verbally, a subject we explore in depth in chapter 10 in connection with prompting legacy. Before we undertake such an important mission, we need to reassure the older person that our communication skills are up to the challenge.

Predictable Encounters

The Predictable Encounters for this chapter challenge us to consider the crucial part played by two nonverbal communication strategies—pauses and the warm-up—in our conversations with senior adults.

Predictable Encounter: Pauses

You are visiting your elderly Aunt Muriel in her apartment at the assisted-living facility you took great care to find for her several years earlier. She invites you to have dinner with her in the communal dining room, but when you arrive, she complains about the quality of the food. Because she has difficulty walking, you are reluctant to suggest a nearby restaurant as an alternative. How should you respond?

- Suggest going to a nearby restaurant anyway.

- Tell her honestly that being with her, not the quality of the food, is the reason for your visit.

- Listen for pauses in her conversation that might signal something else that's upsetting her.

- Ask her what she liked to cook at special family gatherings.

Actually, you might try *all* of these communication options, noting which ones work to get the conversation flowing. It's unclear what she's upset about—probably the quality of the food isn't it—and your challenge is to find out what's bothering her. Suggesting another venue might solve her problem or stimulate a different conversation. Telling her you are more interested in being with her than judging the food might relax her and help her focus attention on you. Observing pauses gives her the control she needs to let what's really troubling her surface. Asking what she would cook if she were able to might bring up subjects she wants to discuss, but does not know how to approach.

All of the options presented above are appropriate ways to handle this particular communication difficulty with this particular elderly relative, but pausing may lead to something significant.

NOW we will learn how to follow up these nonlinear statements with carefully crafted questions that signal we're available to explore the significance of the moment.

Verbal Signals

Crafting Questions: Tone, Attitude, and Those Hidden Messages

A powerful tool in our communication arsenal is the ability to craft and articulate questions. How we probe a person's life determines whether that life gets illuminated and is remembered, or is squelched under the baggage of control issues that refuse to let legacy emerge. Our ability to articulate questions can lead us to a better sense of that legacy, what that person's life was all about and how it affects ours. In essence, we get to discover the pond, the pebbles, and the ripples they created.

Once senior adults open a nonlinear door and indicate a particular path they want to explore, we can signal our willingness to assist by asking the right questions. We can't presume to know the answers; all we can do is gently keep urging the person forward. Sometimes this effort needs more from us than nonverbal reinforcement.

Whether we realize it or not, many of the routine questions we pose every day carry messages, hidden or not, that indicate we doubt our elders' competence. In many cases, we disguise our negative feelings about senior adults' behavior with questions. "Are you going to see the specialist as we agreed?" Our implied challenge to their competence can be perceived as an attempt to wrest control from them and may be met with unexpected and exasperating resistance.

Seniors have learned a fear response to most of our questions through their verbal radar, since typically such questions are an attempt to gain control over their lives and they feel compelled to defend themselves. Poorly crafted questions usually indicate our intention to sniff out the older person's deficits and display our age-based obsession with problem solving. We seem to be asking such questions only to document our elders' inadequacies and lack of preparation for future life events, not to help them cope.

Crafting questions well, on the other hand, gives the older person a clear signal about our openness and sincerity. It's not so much the words we say, but the way we say them—our tone and attitude—that reveal our ability to achieve true communication. Obtaining information from an elderly person requires that we treat them with respect.

Consider the following examples. Note how we would usually question an older person and put ourselves in their position: Which version of the questions below would we rather answer?

A. Dad, why haven't you filled the new prescription the doctor gave you last week?
or
B. Dad, when Uncle Albert developed this condition, I remember he found this particular medication to be quite effective in relieving his symptoms. Do you think it's worth a try?

A. Mr. Jones, have you signed at the bottom of page six yet? Remember we need to submit this document to the IRS by Friday.
or
B. Mr. Jones, it's completely your decision, but the IRS gives us a big tax break for filing this document before the first of the year. Do you want to take advantage of this opportunity to save some money or would you like more time to think about it?

A. Yes, Mom, you've told me all about Aunt Myrtle and how her death affected you. What else is on your mind?
or
B. Of course I know about Aunt Myrtle, Mom, but I never realized how deeply her death affected you. What was your life like before she died?

Which approach affords Dad, Mr. Jones, or Mom the most opportunity to open up and respond? Note that the words are pretty much the same; what's different is the emphasis or tone with which they are said.

How *we ask questions can do one of two things:*

POSITIVE OUTCOME	NEGATIVE OUTCOME
Shore up a person's abilities	Point out deficits
Demonstrate our superior problem-solving abilities	Strike fear in an older person's heart
Partner for solutions	Bulldoze the person into submission
Suggest ways to allow the person to keep control and dignity while indicating the most opportune direction to take	Document inadequacies and poor preparation for life

The words we choose as well as our tone have profound implications when we're dealing with someone who is already under tremendous internal pressure to conduct an extensive life review. We don't need to become our elders' therapists; we do need to develop an ability to choose the right words so that our meaning is clear and supportive.

Various Forms of Questions

Ramping-on Questions

In any conversation, look for an opening in which to share a personal experience about whatever subject the person is referring to, and "ramp-on" by following up with questions that show sincere interest in the content. Decide what the significant theme, event, or experience is and gently ask for more details by referring to a letter, a news event, a change in health, the birth of a child, a death, or any number of life experiences that show commonality with the older person.

How to Say It:

"You've referred to your sister quite a bit. Are you concerned about her in some way?"

"I have heard you mention Agnes a lot. How did you two become friends in the first place? Did you ever think you would be friends all these years?"

"I know what you mean about all those forms. Do you need some assistance in filling them out?"

Perspective Questions

One questioning technique is to offer up our own perspective. This approach appeals to an elderly person's wealth of experience and wisdom. Here are some ways to introduce a difficult subject, or one the person is reluctant to discuss.

How to Say It:

"When I heard about Aunt Helen's latest setback, I asked myself, 'How would I feel if it happened to me?' How do you think she is able to maintain such a positive outlook?"

"Uncle Steve is another issue. I can't imagine him without Aunt Helen. How can I even bring up the subject of what he is going to do once she is gone?"

"What with her career and raising our daughters, Janie is feeling overwhelmed. I help out as much as I can, but I'm worried about her. What do you think about working moms today who are trying to 'have it all'?"

Parallel Circumstances Questions

This style of questioning is particularly helpful when connection with the elderly person has been extremely challenging. A colleague, John, told me of difficulties he'd had communicating with his mom. One day, he went to see her at a time he was extremely harried. Dropping his usual defensiveness at her intrusions into his life, he asked, "Mom," he said, "I have two children whom I love, but I feel as if I'm on a treadmill in caring for them and never have any time to myself. How did you raise four children?" Flattered that he was seeking her advice, she in turn dropped her need to control the conversation and responded in loving, kind, and insightful ways. Notice he didn't challenge her with his notions of child rearing and finding balance in his life; he genuinely was seeking the advice of an older, wiser, and more experienced parent who faced similar challenges and probably had a lot to share on this subject. From that moment on, he told me, they regarded each with less distrust and more caring that opened up many other communication outlets. With that one well-crafted question about their parallel experience of being parents, she dropped her guard and he readily absorbed her invaluable wisdom.

How to Say It:

"Last time we talked, Mr. and Mrs. Timmons were determined to stay in the house where they'd lived for over forty years. What finally made them decide to move into an assisted-living community?"

"My friend Barbara's mother doesn't know what to do about her will. She has three children, a boy and two girls, and she can't figure out how to divvy up the estate. Barbara's brother has never had a real job and lives at home. Barbara and her sister are both successful. How would you sort that one out?"

Interpreting the Answers

Now that we're more savvy about striking the right tone when we ask questions of senior adults, how do we evaluate the answers we hear? Here are some things to listen for as we measure and note responses.

The Warm-up Answer

Many times our first attempts to bring up sensitive topics only produce what I call **warm-up answers**. These are responses that don't invite further conversation. Our best strategy is to drop the subject, because the older person has a clear resistance to it at that particular moment. But remember that the person is processing other possible answers constantly. Bring the subject up again at a later time and see if the person's answer is different. Don't fight the warm-up; if we do, we'll leave the person no room to change his or her mind later on. He'll have no choice but to defend the warm-up answer to the grave, even if his thinking changes. When the person arrives at other answers, and we pick up on and give the right verbal and nonverbal signals that say we are available to listen without judging, the elderly person will provide clues to more meaningful answers.

Warm-up answers are frequently heard after treatment is indicated for a serious medical condition. A friend of mine told me the story of her elderly father who had survived a quadruple bypass several years ago. After a recent checkup, his internist reported that his PSA level was high and suggested a biopsy of his prostate. The father refused, and when my friend and her sister tried to persuade him to "follow doctor's orders," he became adamant about not wanting any treatment whatsoever.

It's natural for a daughter, who loves her father, to want to get the most aggressive treatment available, but consider this situation from his perspective: The father's initial refusal of treatment could be a warm-up answer until he can process the fact that, at age eighty-one, he might have cancer as well as heart disease. He may change his mind and be open to another discussion at a later time. Or, his warm-up answer might be his final thought on the matter: his astute judgment call about how he'd like to spend his remaining years.

How to Say It:

"Dad, making this kind of decision is not easy. The most important thing is, what would give you the best quality of life for the greatest number of years? We will go along and support what you feel is right for you."

"Treatment options are improving all the time. Shall we look at some information on one of those Internet medical sites?"

"If that is what you want to do for now, that's what we'll do for now. Just remember that, as you used to tell me, nothing is cut in stone. If you change your mind tomorrow, then we will help you make that change. We're here for you."

This is how I might have handled my mother during that dark period after my father died and I could not get her to change her will. Instead of urging her—pointedly and frequently—to focus on a task when she had no interest in doing so, I might have given a similar response instead of battling her for control over this matter: "It's okay not to do anything now, but know that I'm here to discuss it when you're ready." Because that's what happened: When she was ready, she told me so, I geared up, and together we got the job done.

This kind of response to a warm-up answer allows control to remain with our senior adults. When there's no fight for control, they are free to focus on what is important. If treatment becomes more important to them, then they will be able to seek it freely, not defensively. Respecting senior adults' boundaries allows them to determine what they feel is important.

Predictable Encounter: The Warm-up

Your elderly father, the one cited earlier who survived open-heart surgery and is now refusing to have a biopsy of his prostate, has been asked by his doctor to sign a waiver indicating he has been advised of treatment options and is refusing them. He is still adamant about not having the biopsy. How do you respond?

- Inform him again of the seriousness of his medical situation.

- Indicate you expect him to go in for treatment.

- Ask him whether he's reconsidered having the biopsy.

- Point out that treatment options are less invasive and painful now than years ago.

While *all* of the four choices listed above are reasonable responses on your part, only by choosing the third option will you determine whether his initial refusal is his warm-up or final answer on this difficult subject. If it's the warm-up, he'll soften his position very slightly and give you room to make a different suggestion. If it's his final answer, then pause, focus on him with interest but not intensity, and wait for him to hear how his answer settles on both of you. If he's adamant, then accept it. But indicate that you are available to listen if he wants to consider a different plan.

The Nonanswer

We ask a question and get some sort of response, but achieve no real meeting of the minds or resolution to the matter. We may wonder whether the older person heard us or understood what we were asking. After seeking assurance that we were understood, we need to interpret such a response as a signal that the person does not wish to discuss the matter further.

How to Say It:

"Mrs. Jones, let me clarify my question. Are you comfortable with this upcoming procedure?"

"Aunt Em, just reassure me that you are set for the weekend."

If we still hear noncommittal responses, we might assume that something of significance is being processed underneath the surface and we must use our legacy-coaching skills to find out what it is.

The Angry Answer

We think we've asked a benign question ("Mom, did you take your medications today?" "Dad, when do you want to schedule that follow-up appointment?") and we get an explosive response. While we might expect this type of reaction from a hormone-driven adolescent, it's quite a shock to hear it from a mature person. Is the person just having a bad day? Being difficult? Or have we brushed up against some sensitive developmental nerves?

An unexpectedly explosive reaction to a routine question signals that the matter is under intense scrutiny in the person's life review. The person may not be reacting to the content of the question we asked. We may have intruded on what the person considers to be a private matter. What we need to do is back off, at least for the time being, and let the person bring the subject up again later.

How to Say It:

"Sorry, Mom. I'll leave those details up to your good judgment."

"Dad, I'm surprised by your reaction, but I accept it. I know you'll make the call when you feel the time is right."

Allowing senior adults to have some breathing room to calm down and collect their thoughts, to figure out for themselves why the question triggered such emotion, is probably our best strategy. When they figure it out, they'll either dismiss such questions as trivial and not worthy of more discussion, or bring up the subject in another context. By backing off, we place control with them—where it belongs!

A Word about the Controlling Individual

Sometimes we come into contact and must interact with elderly individuals who are very controlling and can't seem to let go. My colleague, John, mentioned such difficulties with his mom. We are reluctant to give these individuals more openings to speak or express an opinion than necessary. Going to them for advice is the last thing we want to do, because we don't like their style: They don't discuss an issue, they lecture us.

How do we deal with such individuals? Disarm them. Solicit the personal advice we usually shun and listen intently to their responses. People who are overbearing relax when we defer to their control issues. Usually they soften their tone and become more thoughtful and considerate. To our surprise they may be as knowledgeable as they proclaimed themselves to be and it may be worth giving them the benefit of the doubt. When we do, we open ourselves up to the possibility of being pleasantly surprised.

How to Say It:

"You have grown children who are quite busy with their lives. How do you keep in touch with them?"

"I understand that you were very involved with your parents in their later years. What was your secret for dealing effectively with them?"

Our goal in this chapter has been to heighten awareness of the role we play in enhancing or dousing meaningful conversations with senior adults. We learned that there are certain nonverbal and verbal communication strategies that foster an open and receptive attitude and make us better prepared to handle what surfaces in any conversation. We also learned that observing these signals may make or break our effectiveness in communicating with older persons and that most of us need practice in this area. The good news is that even a small improvement in our skills can yield big results. Remember: Asking the right question in the right way at the right moment can change the course of a life.

Essential Q&A

Q: *How do I determine whether the older person is interested in addressing my concerns after I hear a nonanswer?*

A: The art of crafting questions takes time and testing. Not all of our attempts to salvage a conversation will be successful. Many times we will get perfunctory answers. Other times we will spark real discussions. In between these extremes is where we hone our skills. Our commitment to legacy coaching bids us to listen closely to senior adults to find topics that provide openings. There may be a subtle shift in mood, a return to some particular topic, or a new piece of information. These hints may be new legacy doors waiting to be opened by the right follow-up questions.

Q: Sometimes I ask a really good question but the older person goes off on a completely different topic. Now what do I do?

A: Sometimes secondary subjects that arise are not incidental to the discussion, but the whole deal! When the San Francisco matron stated so forcefully that "doctors don't know everything. Mothers do," I waited and was astonished at where this statement led. She's well known in her community, yet *no one* knew how passionately she felt about the lack of services for special-needs children or how much she needed to talk about it. An innocuous comment about hot weather that prompts a childhood memory of a swimming hole and homemade ice cream begs us to help the senior adult glean legacy value from such a response. Nonlinear statements are among the most important we'll ever hear from our seniors. They beckon us to pick out patterns that indicate where their values may lie.

Q: I am concerned that some of my questions to senior adults may raise strong emotions, such as fear or anger or both. Should I avoid asking such questions?

A: Usually, the more intense the response, the more significant the question we've asked. Emotions are not something to avoid; we must learn to respond to them. Many times these outbursts are gut reactions to topics that have not been aired in the past. If the person appears uncomfortable, don't press for more details at that moment. Validate their feelings ("That sounds like a terrible time in your life.") and move on. If our relationship with the person is solid, and we keep communication channels open, there's a good chance he or she will bring up the subject again in another attempt to understand its significance in the life-review process.

NINE

Returning Control to Its Rightful Owner

*"No man is fit to command another
that cannot command himself."*

—William Penn

Heart Control

I recently interviewed an eighty-year-old woman, Flora, who had a history of heart disease. Two years ago, she stopped follow-up care with her cardiologist, took herself off most of the medications he'd prescribed, and instead started a regimen of vitamins and natural-food supplements. Her medical chart read as if she'd dropped off the face of the earth. From an insurer's point of view, she was difficult to represent because no one knew her current cardiac status.

Because her medical charts were not up-to-date, I needed to interview her to get complete information for her file. When I called her, she sounded at least twenty years younger than her chart indicated—very vital, focused, and energetic—so I said, "It's a little mysterious to me why you stopped seeing your cardiologist."

Flora replied, "Why should I? I'm active, my husband and I take our blood pressure every day and it's normal. I have no symptoms. I feel great! I don't want to go back to the doctor and get a bunch of medications that made me feel sick. They were prescribed for certain conditions and I check those things and all is well."

The message Flora was sending me? "I'm in control and here's the control I insist on having."

Instead of warning her, arguing with her, or dismissing her, I chose to *acknowledge* her decisions. "I understand why you've made these choices. You are exercising control of your health based on what appears to be the most relevant data, which is how you feel, and you are using some objective info: You're not having chest pain or any symptoms, and you have normal blood pressure, so everything appears to be fine."

Was the conversation over? I didn't want it to be, because in order to insure her, I had to persuade her to get a checkup. I continued.

"My only question to you would be: Since you are in such great control of all these conditions, is it possible there are some other factors you may not be aware of and thus may be out of your control?"

"What do you mean? Physical factors or life factors?" Flora's curiosity was piqued.

"My experience in cardiology tells me, based on your history, that while you've been doing very well, heart disease can progress with or without symptoms. Therefore there might be some silent things occurring that could easily be remedied and would still allow you to be in control and lead a very active life. My sense is that you would probably go for the program that would give you ultimate say, because you are a person who is clear about wanting to make decisions where your health is concerned. What I'm wondering is, if there are some silent things going on, wouldn't you want to know about them so you can take control of them again?"

Notice how often I use the word "control" with this eighty-year-old.

Flora asked, "What do you mean?"

"The things that are obvious you understand completely, but I'm referring to silent areas that might be slipping out of control and could start to cause problems. The conditions I'm thinking about aren't merely annoying, they might have serious consequences. Since you sound twenty years younger than you are, and are obviously living life to the fullest, to have your lifestyle diminished by even fifty percent or taken away from you just because you don't have complete information would be a shame."

Flora asked, "What do you think I should do?"

I said, "I'm not sure what you should do, but you might choose to see your cardiologist and have some follow-up tests so he can compare the new numbers with those you had at your last checkup. If you get a good report from the doctor and continue to have great cardiac stability, then you don't have to be concerned. But with your health history, wouldn't you want to be certain that all conditions you can control are being properly treated and that everything is okay?"

She paused. "Well, I don't think I need this."

"You mean a checkup?"

"No," Flora said. "I mean this entire insurance plan. I don't think I need it."

"Okay," I replied. "But here's what I understand from your advisors about your insurance coverage and here's what they think you need to do. It sounds to me what you have now is poorly managed and puts you at a great disadvantage. You have a possibility of choosing a better use of your portfolio and managing your investments to create even more opportunities going forward. And, of course, you may ultimately choose to stay with what you have."

Flora agreed to discuss the matter with her advisor, so I called him and relayed my conversation with her, indicating that control, always an issue with elderly clients, is even more of an issue with someone like this woman who has survived a life-threatening illness. He called her back and went through the revised plan again, frequently using the word "control" to assure her she still was in the driver's seat. After his call, she decided to take the first step and see her doctor.

Flora challenged me on two fronts: First, she said, I have total control over my health and that control must stay with me. I acknowledged that, but pointed out that there may be ways she could *choose* a better approach. And she wanted to hear about that.

Second, she was in total financial control and wanted to stay that way. So I assured her she was, but there were some areas that she could *choose* to improve. She made it clear to me that the decisions she made were not necessarily open to negotiation.

Flora is a senior adult who clearly signaled she needed total control. So I offered language that kept control on her side of the conversation. I used the phrase "poorly managed"—because "manage," "control," and "choose" are all action verbs that seniors respond to.

Suppose the conversation had unfolded a bit differently. Suppose, instead of control language, I offered her logic ("Flora, after a heart attack it's simply common sense to check in with your cardiologist!") or veiled threats ("Flora, we can't consider a revised policy until you get a complete checkup. You must call your doctor right away or we'll lose a great opportunity."). This logical but pressuring language might connect with a baby boomer who needs some prodding to squeeze a doctor visit into an already stuffed calendar, but it works against a senior's need to be in control. If I'd used such language with Flora, I guarantee her answer would have been an emphatic "No!" and that would have been the end of our discussion.

When dealing with seniors, it's important to acknowledge that they have all the control they need in any situation, that they are at the helm, and we aren't interested in usurping their authority.

Reviewing the Repercussions of Loss

Before we discuss Control Rules, we need to pause a moment and recall the source of the urgency and intensity surrounding the need for control. Loss. Arriving from all sides, unabated and unabridged, loss is the persistent reality of aging. We know from chapter 2 the layers of loss the elderly face, yet we cannot overestimate the emotional magnitude of this older-age experience. As legacy coaches we need to develop a clear understanding of this sobering land-scape, a world Bette Davis aptly described as "no place for sissies." Being familiar with the pervasive aspects of loss the elderly face on a daily basis sharpens our appreciation of their control issues. Here are the most important aspects of loss that legacy coaches need to know.

LOSSES ARE UNDENIABLE AND INVADE SENIOR ADULTS' SENSE OF THEMSELVES
In our younger years, losses can be rationalized as momentary setbacks, a de-parture from the norm, something that knocks us off balance but not off track. We are still the same person on the same mission, perhaps sidelined for

a while, but able to adapt to the change the loss presents to our lives. In the elder years, losses attack the very foundation of who we are: our mobility, our worth, and our support group.

How our elders express loss that invades their soul: Because his eyesight has deteriorated, your eighty-something father is no longer able to participate in a weekly golf game that was his ritual for decades. You discover him quietly but openly weeping in his room after you bring him back home from the doctor's office. What do you say to him to acknowledge his profound loss?

How *Not* to Say It:

"Don't fret! There are many other forms of exercise you can still do."

How to Say It:

"I know how important your golf outings were to you. But it's more than just these games you're missing, isn't it?"

LOSSES MOUNT UP LAYER BY LAYER

There is a painful synergy to losses that occur with aging. Our earlier years are marked by single losses: a job, a relationship, or the death of a friend. Older years are marked with layers of loss that magnify the impact of each and every single loss.

How the elderly react to layers of loss: You find your elderly father moping around the house after learning he must undergo a minor surgical procedure. At first he refuses to talk about it, but then he expresses fears about surviving the ordeal. You feel his concerns are blown way out of proportion. What could you say to him that would encourage him to talk about other losses, as well as this one?

How *Not* to Say It:

"Come on, Dad. Buck up. This surgery is no big deal."

How to Say It:

"I know it's hard to keep going in the face of all these setbacks. How can I help you regain a sense of balance?"

LOSSES CAN OCCUR IN RAPID-FIRE SEQUENCE, WITH LITTLE OR NO RECOVERY TIME BETWEEN EACH

The losses we sustain in our younger years are generally spread out, with ample recovery periods. In older years the losses begin to come in clusters without the benefit of any recovery time. Sometimes they provoke a domino effect, with one loss causing another, then another (for example, a broken hip that leads to convalescent care and sale of the family home).

How our elders react to a cluster of losses: Your Aunt Bea complains loudly and often, "I just can't walk anymore!" but when you visit her, she gets around just fine, albeit slowly, with the aid of a walker. What can you say that would acknowledge her loss of mobility?

How *Not* to Say It:

"Yes, it's hard to rely on a walker, but you always have a way of bouncing back!"

How to Say It:

"I understand how devastating this loss of mobility is. Talk to me about ways you are limited in your daily activities. I want to help you figure out how to cope."

Once we understand our elders' struggle with daily losses, we can adapt a few general communication strategies to their specific developmental need. The legacy coach approach seeks to put control issues to rest to minimize friction with this age group and allow them to focus on other significant developmental tasks.

Control Rules

Acknowledging the Magnitude of Loss

These communication rules for managing control issues illuminate the magnitude of the battle senior adults face in trying to respond to their developmental mandate. Our responses to these situations can undermine or support them in this endeavor. Acknowledging in every conversation that we understand how powerful the control driver is will improve communication immeasurably. When we've struck the right chord, we see our elders visibly and verbally relax. Control rules *always* apply; they never take a holiday.

ULTIMATUMS NEVER WORK

With this (and most other) age groups, ultimatums usually backfire. Don't use them.

How *Not* to Say It:

"*Mom, make up your mind! We're going to be late.*"

How to Say It:

"*Mom, I think either hat works with that outfit. Which feels like you today?*"

STAND BY YOUR ELDERS!

Elderly people need reassurance we won't abandon them or question their decision once they make it—even if we don't agree on the issue. Our consistent support is especially important when medical treatments are suggested. Sometimes the elderly don't want to have invasive treatments, particularly if they've survived other life-threatening illnesses. Accept and respect their decision not to seek treatment for a new ailment.

Remember that senior adults need control to pout, ponder, obsess, and take a stand. Legacy coaches allow them the freedom to express these reactions without getting annoyed and withdrawing. In the world of legacy coaching, abandoning senior adults is not an option. We need to assure them we will discuss the matter further whenever they are ready to do so.

How *Not* to Say It:

"*Mom, a breast biopsy is so routine! Don't give it a second thought.*"

How to Say It:

"*Mom, you know what's best for you and, if you'd like, I'll help you explain your thinking to the doctor.*"

GIVE THE ELDERLY ROOM TO CHANGE THEIR MINDS

Let our elders know that whatever decision they make we'll support, but leave the door open for revised decision making. We want to create a comfort zone where they'll be able to come to us without losing face if they change their minds.

How *Not* to Say It:

"If that's what's you've decided, then I guess that's all there is to it!"

How to Say It:

"I'm not sure I would have made that call, but I accept your decision. If you'd ever like to revisit this issue, I'll be happy to discuss it again."

If senior adults seem invested in a decision and unwilling to discuss the matter further, we need to determine if we've backed them into a corner. If we modify our conversational approach by acknowledging their viewpoint and assuring them they have all the control they need ("Of course you're in control." "These decisions are right for you." "You certainly have the authority to stick with that plan."), then we give them room to change their minds.

WATCH YOUR TONE

Elderly people are sensitive to an authoritarian tone that can creep into our conversations with them. We're not lawyers cross-examining someone on the witness stand. Legacy coaches acknowledge the elderly person's perspective, even when we don't agree with it. Failure to do so feels to this age group like confrontation, as if we're lecturing or talking down to them, rather than trying to communicate.

How *Not* to Say It:

"Didn't I warn you that you'd confuse all those little pills? You must use the daily reminder pill box the doctor gave you."

How to Say It:

"I'm glad we nipped this situation in the bud! Let's sort next week's meds the way the doctor suggested."

WAIT FOR THE REAL MESSAGE

The initial response of an elderly person to an important question may not be an honest one. Because of such factors as fatigue, loneliness, or confusion, seniors may want to placate or cooperate as a way of maintaining contact and control. If we press them on an issue, they can become obstinate and we realize their cooperation isn't heartfelt. Be alert to the fact that expressions of control can be uneven.

How *Not* to Say It:

"What do you mean you don't want to go? I went through a lot of trouble to get these tickets."

How to Say It:

"You seem hesitant about using these tickets. Why?"

CONSIDER "NO!" THE WARM-UP ANSWER

Particularly with medical procedures, the first "no" could be the warm-up answer. After surviving a serious illness, a person would not immediately be able to summon the energy to deal with another setback. Wait a few days, then introduce the subject again. If their answer varies, we know their initial response was the warm-up and that we have an opening to discuss new procedures.

How *Not* to Say It:

"I can't understand why you won't get that X-ray. It takes five minutes, it's painless, and it'll tell us a lot."

How to Say It:

"That certainly is a decision you can make today."

A CHANGE IN DIRECTION MAY REVEAL SOMETHING ELSE OF SIGNIFICANCE

If an older person looks as if he or she is moving forward, then heads in a different direction, that new direction may be triggered, unpredictably and mysteriously, by a different control issue that forces the person to change course. Much as a revealed move in chess opens up other possibilities for play, an elderly person's change in direction has the potential to open up entirely new subjects for conversation. Ask if there's another matter the person wants to air.

How *Not* to Say It:

"But yesterday you were perfectly happy with these arrangements."

How to Say It:

"I thought these matters were settled. Did I misunderstand or has something else occurred to you that you'd like to discuss?"

EXPLOSIVE RESPONSES SIGNAL UNRESOLVED CONTROL ISSUES

Volcanic expressions of anger come out of the blue. For example, our offer to help Mom fill out her income-tax forms makes her go ballistic. Any issue can trigger an explosion; any interaction can escalate from a skirmish into a major conflict. We can't always predict what topic is going to result in an emotional outburst, but when we hear a loud protest to an innocent statement, it's likely we've tapped a nerve and exposed an important control issue that is currently gripping the person's psyche.

This is a scene I witnessed in the grocery store checkout line one afternoon:

> *Baby-boomer daughter (kindly):* "Mom, just put your items in my basket and we'll sort them out later."
> *Seventy-plus mom (angrily):* "Guess I'm not competent enough to buy my own groceries anymore!"

The daughter was taken aback at her mother's reaction. Her intention was to move quickly through the line; her mother reacted as if the daughter were judging her ability to provide for her family. The daughter, to her credit, realized she may have tapped into her mother's unspoken feelings about a profound sense of loss of the independence that once allowed her to shop and make menu decisions on her own.

How *Not* to Say It:

"Mom, please, let's not have a scene."

How to Say It:

"Oh, Mom, I was merely trying to speed things along. Here, then, why don't you go ahead of me?"

How to Say It *Later*:

"Mom, what was it about my offer to pay for your groceries that upset you so much?"

Unless the issue involves an immediate threat to life or safety, quickly return control to the elderly person. Any resistance to a suggestion we make signals that the senior adult is dealing with control issues that may need more discussion.

BE PATIENT WITH THE DETAILS

Our elders can focus on unimportant details, with much fretting and indecision that many people find irritating. They can also arrive at conclusions to situations or decisions about unimportant matters that surprise us. If we question those decisions, they can overreact and shut us out for a while. How can we break through a stony exterior and get to the heart of the matter?

How *Not* to Say It:

"Uncle George, really, it's not the end of the world!"

How to Say It:

"I understand what you must be feeling. It's so hard to put these things into perspective, isn't it?"

KEEP YOUR PERSPECTIVE

Don't get hung up on a small event. It just creates more skirmishes and in the long run isn't worth the battle.

How *Not* to Say It:

"You knew I was coming to visit today. Why didn't you mention you used up all your prescriptions?"

How to Say It:

"I see you've run out of your prescriptions. Would you like me to re-fill them now or before I leave?"

Control Tools

What do these Control Rules above have in common? Almost every legacy-coach response uses one or more of the three Control Tools: action verbs, the right verb and not the wrong one, and our imaginary business cards. Examples below show how these tools work.

The Power of the Action Verb

Action verbs, particularly ones on my A-list below, offer control to senior adults. Use these verbs as often as possible by working them into any conversation with an elderly person.

THE A-LIST OF ACTION VERBS
Administer, choose, command, conduct, control, create, decide, direct, elect, embrace, espouse, guide, handle, lead, maintain, manage, opt, order, organize, overlook, pick, plan, rule, select, settle, steer, supervise, take the helm, vote.

Using these verbs places control squarely in the hands of the person we are talking with. If that person happens to be elderly, these words are comforting and appeal to that basic need to have mastery over life's events at a time when control in many areas is slipping away.

These verbs shout to older adults that they retain the right to choose any direction, make any decision they wish—that they are fully in charge.

The Right Verb versus the Wrong Verb

Control, direct, guide, lead, manage, organize, run. If we compare those action control-focused verbs to verbs such as **transfer, grant, give,** and **assign,**

what do we have? To those citizens born in the Depression, who later had to sacrifice family and prosperity during the fierce World War II years, and then had to rebuild their lives and raise their families by scrimping and saving and investing wisely, the second set of verbs sounds like "free." Particularly in the financial-planning arena, verbs like "transfer" and "assign" are alien notions to senior adults and go against their developmental agendas. This is the generation that Tom Brokaw writes about in *The Greatest Generation*. As a group, they worked hard for everything they have. They usually resist the notion of giving anything to anyone who hasn't earned it. Avoid such verbs.

In the following discussion between a financial planner and his elderly client, consider the statement the senior would be more likely to respond to.

How *Not* to Say It:

"Mr. Jones, we need to transfer these assets to your children now to avoid a big hit by the IRS later."

How to Say It:

"Mr. Jones, one way to maintain control over these assets is to create a plan for your children that assures growth for many years to come."

If we don't understand the difference in nuance in those two statements, we don't understand the developmental mandates of the elderly. To an elderly person, "transferring" money to anyone sounds as if the recipient is getting a free ride, something most elderly people would never condone. *Maintaining control* over money that in turn continues to *create* opportunities for a future generation taps into senior adults' needs to both feel in control *and* be remembered.

Outside the financial arena, the same powerful verbs need to be used. For instance, in the two comments below between a daughter and her elderly father in precarious health, which would be a legacy coach's approach?

How *Not* to Say It:

"Dad, Dr. Smith has been following you for years. If he says it's time to retest you, then that's what you need to do."

How to Say It:

"Dad, I understand your desire to control the number of tests you take. You may change your mind in a few days, and whenever you give us the go-ahead, we'll direct the doctor to schedule the tests he says you need."

"Here's My Imaginary Business Card"

The closer the relationship we have with our elders, the easier this tool is to use. Some elderly people feel overwhelmed and need to hear us say to them, "How can I help you stay in control of this situation?" or "What part can I play in helping you maintain control here?" Being direct often allows us to approach difficult discussions.

This technique works particularly well when an elderly person is passive. Communicating with an unassertive, unassuming person is tricky, because the way that personality style tends to exercise control is through indecision, not by acknowledging that any solution we suggest is satisfactory. By handing them our imaginary business card, we indicate we are willing to facilitate them at the time and under the circumstances of *their* choosing.

How *Not* to Say It:

"Let's review and resolve this plan by next Thursday."

How to Say It:

"What is your plan for managing/directing/organizing this situation?" If they don't have a plan, suggest one. If they start to describe something that seems unwieldy or unrealistic, jump in and say, "Is there any part of this plan that I can help you control?" or "I'd like to jump in here and figure this out with you. If now is not a good time, may I leave my 'imaginary' business card with you [or a similar statement conveying that control is with them, but your door is wide open] so you can contact me in the future?"

There is no better way to allow senior adults to stay on top of any situation than to give them our imaginary business cards, verbal reassurance we offer assistance when they need it.

Essential Q&A

Q: My mom and I have never seen eye to eye. My view is that she's a very controlling person, so the idea of reinforcing that behavior doesn't sit well with me. Would offering her control, using those action verbs, actually work with her personality type?

A: Yes, definitely. Even if your mom has no trouble leading the brigade, she's still looking for a sign that you recognize her right to do so. Part of our conflict with controlling people is that we tend to fight them for the very thing they won't surrender. Don't fight your mom anymore; rather, acknowledge she has all the control she wants. Offer her control language at every opportunity. When she realizes there's nothing to fight about, she's likely to relax and have more honest, open discussions on a variety of subjects.

Q: While I agree that my eighty-year-old dad has a right to refuse medical treatment, I worry that his condition will deteriorate and I won't forgive myself for not trying harder to persuade him to seek help while I had the chance. What can I say to him about seeing the doctor if he refuses to go on his own?

A: Sometimes an elderly person's initial refusal to seek medical treatment is a warm-up answer. Wait a few days and mention the subject again by offering your dad complete control of the decision, the timing, and extent of further testing. If he refuses, assure him you accept his decision. If he asks more questions about the procedure, supply him with the answers without pressuring him to make an appointment. He's indicating he is willing to reconsider and needs to be facilitated, so raise the issue again a few days later using the same control language as before.

Understand that your concern about your dad's deteriorating condition is not his problem. He's lived a long life and in reviewing it, he may have decided he's lived long enough. It's a subject seniors in compromised health review every day. It clashes with our age group's developmental drivers that compel us to take charge and resolve matters, but remember, we don't yet know what it's like to be old and need to respect our elders' decisions, even if we find them painful and don't agree with them.

Q: How many times in conversations with an elderly person should I use the word "control"?

A: Both nonprofessionals and professionals should use the word "control" and its A-list of synonyms as often as possible. You will be amazed at the verbal and nonverbal responses you get. You'll observe elderly people relax and be more open to discussing any issue you want to raise.

Q: My parents don't realize they need more help doing simple tasks around the house, such as cleaning, cooking, and maintenance. Whenever I bring up the subject, they refuse to discuss it and dismiss my concerns. They mutter something about privacy and do not want "strangers" with them "constantly." How do I bring up the subject again so they'll hear me out?

A: Offer the language of control. For example, you might say, "Dad, it's completely *your decision*, but you know I've mentioned that it's getting more difficult for you and Mom to maintain the house. What kind of assistance do you think *you* both can *manage?* Can I help *you create* a schedule for a helper that won't interfere with your activities? If *you* had to *create* a résumé of the ideal person to assist you, what kind of experience would *you envision* for the person *you hire?*"

This kind of language—using active verbs that place seniors at the helm— will offer your parents control of the situation. They'll relax and be able to think things through in a more focused, less defensive way.

THIS chapter outlined communication strategies that allow seniors to feel in control of their lives at a time when they're dealing with mounting losses. If we master the art of allowing our elders to push the control buttons, we find them responding in new ways that facilitate both of our age-based agendas. With less conflict, they relax and their conversations become somewhat easier. We begin to feel like heroes in their eyes. Why? Because we've freed them to focus on their other equally compelling developmental task: the search for the way they wish to be remembered.

TEN

Discovering Organic Legacy

---

*"What lies behind us and what lies before us are small matters
compared to what lies within us."*

—*Ralph Waldo Emerson*

From the Heroic to the Transformational

There is no more important job associated with legacy coaching than helping our elders determine how they will be remembered. In fact, earning their trust that allows us this privilege is the goal of becoming a legacy coach. Legacy coaches employ a few simple yet powerful communication techniques that prompt our elders to review their lives. When this process begins, we need to listen for the values seniors express in almost every conversation. Those values provide the keys to their unfolding legacy.

The prompting techniques are easy to learn; the answers we hear are sometimes difficult to assess. But if we're alert, compassionate, and committed, a marvelous world opens up that allows us to explore the transformational possibilities inherent in this process. As the elderly person's *organic legacy* unfolds, it becomes the heartfelt connection between generations past and all that are to follow.

How do we know if the life-review process that leads to legacy is under way? Is it possible to determine how far in the process our loved one, client, or colleague is? Just how much facilitation does any one person need? We need to begin at the beginning, assuming nothing.

The Legacy Quilt

Think of a person's *organic legacy* as an enormous quilt created not from scraps of cloth material, but from moments of emotional material gathered from a lifetime of memories, examined for content, quality, and values, reexamined from the perspective of old age, then sewn together into an enveloping garment that reflects the values the person holds most dear: his or her essential perceptions, memories, and truths that must be passed along to future generations.

A pretty tall order, we might say, but the search for organic legacy goes on with us or without us. It is a continual assessment performed by anyone who lives to be a certain age. As legacy coaches, we want to be part of this process.

Organic legacy is the unique footprint we want to leave for our time on earth. We all live unique lives. Some are more colorful and complex than others, but they are all interesting and worthy of our utmost consideration. Therefore, we all have the *potential* to have a unique legacy. Unfortunately, that potential can remain unrealized because the discovery process can be derailed, defeated, or overwhelmed by the demands of aging—losses, poor health, unrelenting battles for control—and some of us die without much assistance in getting this job done.

As a culture, we tend not to place enough emphasis on the skills needed to mine our organic legacies. As we learned in chapter 3, if not facilitated, we may be remembered only by default, leaving a legacy we had no part in shaping. Or we may simply have "done the right thing" by our survivors, but a political legacy may not be our heartfelt one.

How do we tap into this life-review process and ensure that our elders leave their own individual footprint as proof that they lived? Is it possible to determine how far seniors have come in shaping organic legacy? If we suspect there's work to be done, how do we reinvigorate their search?

Legacy Rules

Let's review the rules about how an *organic legacy* is created before we learn some simple strategies to facilitate it.

Legacy is not optional. When understood as a developmental need, legacy insists on being addressed, either consciously or unconsciously. It's the end product of life review, a developmental mandate of those privileged to survive into old age. Once we enter this stage, we constantly reconsider our lives to determine how we want to be remembered.

Returning to the past is not pathology. Life review and the creation of a legacy are a natural evolution of where we need to be developmentally at the end of our lives.

Legacy surfaces when control issues abate. If control issues are not resolved, they dominate our developmental mandate and we never get to focus on legacy.

In searching for an *organic legacy*, events that may have been misinterpreted, misunderstood, or unrepaired in the past are reexamined. This process reinterprets events and, if necessary, invites us to make amends. This process is difficult because of many factors:

- the number of experiences we have stored up over a lifetime;

- the tremendous mental focus needed to do it right;

- the physical energy required to remain highly involved at a time when physical strength is ebbing each day;

- unfacilitated control issues.

Creation of an *organic legacy* offers the potential for healing. Forming an *organic legacy* means that we have dedicated considerable time, energy, and insight into what has happened in our lives and tried to determine what everything means. Packaging the essence of that journey provides future generations with a prospective that fosters understanding, forgiveness, acceptance, and resolution of values that may or may not have been appreciated during our lifetimes.

Legacy is not simply a summary of what we've experienced. Part of our legacy is what we lived and part of it is what we may not have lived, but what we admired. Both parts of legacy contain values for which we would like to be remembered. Legacy coaches facilitate both of these needs.

Legacy gives us a chance to play an active role in the future. Through *organic legacy* we are able to create a vehicle that has the potential to influence people beyond those we encountered during our lifetime. The goal is to be part of a conversation one hundred years from now, even though we are not physically present, because we set in motion a series of events or memories that live on after us.

Legacy Tools

The stronger our relationship with the older generation, the easier it is to facilitate the legacy process. The weaker the relationship, the more frustrated we tend to become with our elders' attempts to communicate. Our message in facilitating legacy: I want to understand you better. I am strong enough to help you confront the losses you've endured and mistakes you may have made, and not consider you to be weak. In fact, your review of those losses makes you appear seasoned and heroic in my eyes.

Knowing how important our legacy coach role is, how do we then facilitate life review in our elders? The first step is to determine where the senior adult is in this complex process. Once we determine that, we can use one of four communication strategies to open legacy doors and find out more.

Clues and Accelerators

In determining where a person is in the legacy process, pay close attention to these clues and accelerators.

A change in circumstances can intensify the search. Many things, especially the loss of a friend or spouse, can accelerate life review. An older adult, who might have been indifferent to or defensive about questions touching on the past, may be more responsive while dealing with the aftermath of loss. We need to renew our efforts when seniors face new realities.

Loss of health can change everything. We need to assess the state of senior adults' health, both physical and psychological. Once health starts to decline, that is, when a person moves from the "lasting" to the "leaving" zone, or what Mary Pipher in *Another Country* calls moving from the young-old to the old-old stages of life, the life-review process takes on new urgency. The young-old are still healthy and vigorous. They may have a few chronic medical conditions, but the problems are not debilitating and routine medical care keeps pain and other symptoms in check. Once health becomes a chronic problem, however, a person's entire mental and emotional landscape changes, and we begin to hear statements such as the ones below.

How *They* Say It:

"I guess that's the last time I'll be able to make the trip to the lake."
"I am not sure how many more birthdays I will be around to celebrate."
"I want to see the sunset on the ocean just one more time."
"Who will take care of all this stuff when I'm no longer here?"
"I don't want to be a burden to my son when I die."
"I hope you will remember me."

The elderly are signaling clearly that life review has shifted into high gear. At this point, they may feel an overwhelming need to make sense out of what has occurred and the focus on the past becomes almost obsessive. To each of these statements, our legacy-coach approach is to determine what they are trying to convey—a need to share memories, a desire to see familiar places once more, an interest in mending a relationship—and why that desire is so compelling.

How to Say It:

Ask gently but directly what it is the person is remembering and try to determine what value may need to be articulated:

"When did you make your first trip to the lake? Who were you with?"
"What was your best birthday ever? Why?"
"Do you want to take a ride to the ocean this weekend?"
"What things mean the most to you? What do you want to happen with those items?"
"My grandma said the same thing to my mother. She never was a burden to my mom."
"How would you like me to remember you?"

Listen to their responses: If they haven't figured out that piece of their life review, they won't hesitate to go into more detail, agree with your suggestions, or refine your request. Listen for series of values through *repeated* and detailed themes, people, and events.

Signals and Hints

Old age is a look back. Ironically, in old age, in order to go forward, we must look back. We're not prepared to do it because every previous stage has been propelling us forward. Looking back isn't the need to erect a monument so we'll be remembered. It's a profound need to make sense out of what has occurred and assign meaning to it. It is a need to come to terms with our life.

Certain phrases signal that the seniors are recontextualing their lives. Their tone and emphasis on these phrases provide hints about the urgency and importance of what is being revealed.

How *They* Say It:

"*I never understood her anger* until now."
"I don't think I ever *appreciated how important that was to you.*"
"I thought *you* always *knew* . . ."
"*I have* not *thought about him* in years!"
"Out of nowhere, *I suddenly remembered the time when* . . ."
"*I was so upset* at the time, but *it all seems so silly* now."
"I never told *your father* how much *that meant to me.*"
"Where is *Billy* now? *Do you think he'd be willing to drop by for a chat?*"

How *They* Say It:

What looked like a defeat, a loss, a disaster, a wrong road taken, in a recontextualized world becomes something very different.

First, the elderly need breathing space to gather up experiences. ("Now that he's gone, I can say . . .")
Second, they have to rethink what the experiences mean. ("I never understood . . .")

Third, they need help in deciding how those experiences fit into what they feel their lives have come to represent. ("Why am I thinking about that person now?")

Responding to the Signals

Learning how to develop the older person's question through the use of a "response question" is a primary legacy-coach skill. Sometimes no response is the proper one, but usually attentive listening is the key. We may have been taught never to respond to a question with a question, but in legacy work, it is an effective and nurturing tool. For example, to statements indicating the person is working toward a new resolution, toward healing, we could respond this way:

How to Say It:
"Why does her anger look different now?"
"What changed your mind?"
"What made you think I knew you felt that way?"
"What is your favorite memory about him?"
"What was that time like? Who were the most important people in your life?"
"Why does that situation look different now?"
"What are your favorite memories of Dad?"
"When was the last time you saw Billy? Would you like me to locate his number so you can call him?"

The Art of Asking Development Questions

As noted in chapter 9, the way we ask the same question can elicit very different responses. Legacy coaches use development questions. Development questions seek more than facts, they seek context and emotion. They open doors; they invite experiential browsing. Compare the difference below between fact-finding and development questions.

How to Say It:

Fact: "What was your dad's name?"
Development Question: "What was your dad like?"

Fact: "Father's cause of death?"
Development Question: "How did your life change after your father died?"

Fact: "How many siblings do you have?"
Development Question: "Do you get along with your brothers and sisters?"

Development questions invite the older person to reach deep into an experience to bring it to life. An accomplished legacy coach can transform fact-finding into value-finding queries. Answers to value-finding questions bring us closer to the emotional material buried beneath layers of lifetime experience.

Uncovering the "Secret Stuff"

Legacy coaches want to know the "secret stuff," emotional material that contains the values to be threaded through the person's legacy quilt. Sometimes our efforts will meet with a resounding thud at best, hostility or dogma at worst. Expect setbacks, but don't give up.

In order to get to the "secret stuff"—the value-laden material—we sometimes need to start in the safety of the conversational suburbs and work in toward the core of the person's experience. Sometimes this strategy requires nothing more than our ability to remain silent and aware of the "hiccup" in their conversation—a pause, a repetition—that signals an important value has just been, or is about to be, revealed, and knowing how to respond appropriately. But sometimes more proactive facilitation is needed. That's when it's important to employ one or more of four different communication strategies that will not only spark life review and recontextualization, but enhance our ability to interpret what we hear.

Below are five communication strategies for prompting life review:

- ask open-ended core questions

- harvest responses to open-ended questions

- listen for the values

- note the legacy vehicles

- start with "Tell me about . . ."

These simple strategies, complete with examples, are described below.

Legacy Strategy 1: Ask Open-ended Core Questions

Open-ended questions spark the search for organic legacy. The questions are open-ended, because the answers don't seek facts. They rely on interpretation, memory, and values. **Since the same question can elicit different responses on different days, there are no right or wrong answers. In fact, as the elderly re-contextualize patches of memory that are forming their legacy quilt, answers should differ.** An attentive legacy coach helps them stitch together these fragments into a coherent and meaningful whole.

Below is a portfolio of core open-ended questions that can be used in the discovery of legacy. These examples are mere suggestions. Think of others tailored to the experiences of the senior adults you know. Listen for the values they express in almost every sentence of their answers.

How to Say It:

"What is your earliest memory?"

"What was the world like when you grew up?"

"What do you remember about your grandparents?"

"In what ways are you like your mother?"

"In what ways are you like your father?"

"What was the most significant event of your childhood?"

"Who was the most significant person in your life when you were growing up?"

"What were your family's greatest strengths?"
"What was the biggest obstacle your family had to overcome?"
"What was your favorite childhood dream?"
"Who was your best friend when you were growing up?"
"Who was your favorite teacher?"
"How did you meet your spouse?"
"In what ways do you complement each other?"
"In what ways are you different from one another?"
"Who is the most significant person in your life?"
"What has been the happiest time of your life?"
"What do you consider your greatest accomplishment?"
"What do your consider your greatest disappointment?"
"If you could change anything at any time in your life, what would it be?"
"What are you most thankful for?"

Legacy Strategy 2: Harvest Responses to Open-ended Questions

Look attentive, but say nothing. Very often the most appropriate responses to these open-ended questions are emotional and physical—attentive listening—not verbal. It's not in the elder person's interest for us to fill in the blanks, supply a missing detail, or correct a memory that doesn't jibe with ours. We're attempting to let them air their version of events, not incorporate ours.

Reinforce the value or theme expressed. Sometimes the best response is another open-ended question that invites the elderly to elaborate on something they've just expressed.

How to Say It:

"What about Aunt Miriam impressed you the most?"
"What do you think will happen to Sally if she remarries?"
"Why do you think your granddaughter should stay home and raise her child?"

Listen for repeated details, people, or entire stories. Do the details change with each retelling? Are they vivid? Is the narrator a hero in the story or a victim?

Fulfilled or bereft? Excited or sad? What we think we hear is probably correct: Legacy coaches test their hunches by asking these kinds of follow-up questions:

How to Say It:

"So Uncle Harry's action in this matter irritated you?"
"How would you have acted differently?"
"How did his actions affect other events in your life?"
"How were you able to cope with such a loss?"
"What would you do about it if you could?"

Answers to these questions reveal the values for which the person wants to be remembered.

Legacy Strategy 3: Listen for the Values

My colleague, Sally, recently found herself chatting after a dinner party with her fiancé's eighty-four-year-old aunt. This elderly woman, known to her as Aunt Ruth, had visited the cemetery that afternoon to honor the anniversary of her older sister and only sibling's death, but now they were surrounded by the antics of Ruth's grandchildren, who were having a wonderful time staying up late and showing off before an appreciative audience. During a lull, Aunt Ruth expressed to Sally how emotional she'd become at the grave site; she loved her sister and missed her dearly. "I'm the oldest member of my family now," she remarked. "There's no one left alive who knew my parents. It's a terribly empty feeling."

Sally was amazed! What she observed in Aunt Ruth was an elderly woman in excellent health, still happily married, and very much loved by her children and grandchildren. Sally, familiar with seniors' needs to review their lives, didn't know Aunt Ruth well and wasn't sure how to respond to this woman's heartfelt expression of "emptiness" in the midst of what seemed like an abundance of family connection. Sally asked a variety of questions, but Aunt Ruth herself provided a clue to her legacy when she asked Sally, "And what was your parents' trade?"

Recognizing her opening, Sally answered briefly, then asked the same question of Aunt Ruth—and for the two next hours heard in great detail how this woman valued her remarkable parents: Her father escaped from a prison camp in

Siberia ("He was from an educated, rather well-off Russian family, but he got into some political trouble.") and arrived in this country in 1908 with no family, no connections, and knowing no English. Her mother worked at home as a seamstress until her children were in school, then worked in the sweatshops. What, in fact, was her father's trade? "He was an intellectual but, to earn a living, became a house painter," she replied, then went on: "I got a job as a secretary when I graduated high school at age sixteen, and went to college at night. It took me eight years to get my first degree, and I became a teacher, then an administrator."

Listen to the values this woman absorbed from her parents! While Sally found the details of this woman's life interesting, she was more impressed with Ruth's need to review what she holds most dear—the value of hard work, education, and family. Clearly these are values she was taught, by which she lived her life, and for which she wants to be remembered.

Once we learn to listen with legacy-coach ears—"I'm now the oldest one in my family. . . . I have no one to talk to who knew my parents. . . . It's an empty feeling."—and ask the right questions, we can hear the values for which seniors want to be remembered, the ones they need to fashion into their legacy quilts. Because these values infuse every conversation, there is ample opportunity to forge meaningful connections.

AS we think back over Ruth's story and others in previous chapters, what values were expressed? Once we discern them, how do we promote their full expression as the person tries to shape a meaningful legacy?

Before we attempt to facilitate this process, we need to understand what this older generation treasures most.

The dominant values of what Tom Brokaw calls the "greatest generation" are what Mary Pipher highlights in her book *Another Country*, which bear repeating in light of our attempts to facilitate life review. Dr. Pipher notes that members of the seventy-plus generation are the last to have grown up in a communal society, where families lived close together, neighbors knew and relied on each other, and people resided in the same neighborhoods their entire lives. These are the families that endured the ravages of the Depression, with its lost opportunities and very little income, as well as the rationing and other deprivations of World War II. When they married, this generation scrimped and saved to provide their children—the baby boomers—all the advantages they rarely enjoyed: music lessons, summer camp, a college education.

If we understand the core values of our seniors, we will begin to hear those values surface in almost every conversation. When I was a college student, my grandmother told me a story from her childhood about a couple in her neighborhood who died in a tragic accident and left behind two young children. "What happened to those children?" I asked. "Why, we took them in, of course!" she stated, looking at me as if I had suddenly gone mad. There could be no other answer to my question, her emphatic reply informed me, and her gaze said she clearly regarded me as a person upon whom the values of a communal society were lost.

Loss of the communal society has profound ramifications on the lives of our elders. What is also a fact is that the surviving members of that generation still hold its values near their core. We need to be aware of those values in order to facilitate life review.

How do we discern values in a story we hear? When someone recounts an experience, that person is relaying actions by characters in a story. And those characters are doing certain things that are either noble or not. These characters reflect the ability for self-sacrifice and dedication and loyalty, or they don't. Listen for the values in those behaviors that represent something beyond self-serving interests. Or listen for the opposite of those characteristics—bitterness, anger, and disappointment.

"I did this and after all the loyalty I showed, they were dishonest, disloyal." This kind of statement signals that the person values traits that were *not* displayed.

"Her husband was sick for twenty years. And for twenty years she did the grocery shopping, took care of him, raised their kids." What are the values in that statement? Profound loyalty. Dedication. Sense of duty. Good work ethic. Statements like this one offer clues to a person's legacy. After all, the more we engage our elders in conversation, the better we become in discerning the values they hold most dear.

How to Say It:

This is how to respond to value-laden statements. Acknowledge the values we hear from our seniors by asking for more information.

"How has your life reflected some of those values?"
"In what way have those values become part of your life?"
"How would you like your legacy to reflect some of these things?"

Defining a senior adult's values is crucial. Whether he or she lived up to those values is beside the point. If that value is what the person admired, that's the way he or she wants to be remembered.

Legacy Strategy 4: Note the Legacy Vehicles

Legacy coaches need to listen for what I call "legacy vehicles," which also provide clues to the values a person needs to pass on to future generations. Legacy vehicles can be any of the following:

- Acts of courage

- Decisions to forgive or repair a relationship

- Reflection on such questions as "Have I been a good parent, friend, boss?" "Have I done enough for others?" "Have I contributed to my community?"

- Impact of declining health

- Family stories

We may be quite familiar with the acts of courage to which our elders now refer. We may have begged our elder to reconcile with a family member for years and doubt their sincerity now. We may have heard that family story a dozen times. We sometimes get frustrated with them, because they seem so focused on their health.

Actually, such conversations are a huge gift to us, because they open up legacy doors! We need to listen to these statements with new appreciation, because at the end of life, they become vehicles for memories that need a different response. For example, when our elders talk about health, they are giving us entrée to their core values. Their back hurts? Ask them to describe the pain, then listen to what other subjects may arise. They're repeating a family story we've heard dozens of times? We need to listen for the telling detail we've never heard before. Aunt Em wants to make contact with her estranged son? What is it about establishing contact that seems so important now?

These legacy vehicles are opportunities for us to highlight values a person needs to explore.

Legacy Strategy 5: Start with "Tell Me About . . ."

One of the most powerful phrases in our communication arsenal is this invitation to relate a story. "Tell me about . . ." is particularly useful for legacy coaches facilitating the life-review process. This phrase is the medical equivalent of "What's going on?" (Anything can be going on, not necessarily medical.) The legal equivalent is: "What's the most important thing for me to know about you?"

As legacy coaches, using "tell me about . . ." statements helps us probe. For example, to a relative we could say: "Tell me about my mom when she was little." "Tell me about my dad as a young man." "Tell me about growing up in Grandma's old house."

"Tell me about . . ." always rings a legacy bell. It's a big verbal driver that evokes the oral tradition. The "tell me about . . ." command signals to seniors that we're listening, interested in what they have to say, and want to hear more.

Don't forget to start with general themes to reach the core of the person's experience, an excellent technique for establishing rapport and building trust when we sense recontextualization is occurring. If the person is having trouble finding significance in the legacy vehicle, "tell me about . . ." is a way to approach the subject from a different direction and perhaps stimulate a different response.

Refining Our Role as Legacy Coach

Below is a checklist for legacy coaches to help with the process of recontextualizing our seniors' experiences. Informed by the strength of our commitment to and relationship with the older person, we can begin with those organic connectors in that person's nonlinear world and start to gather scenes that are important. This process, once mastered, is one we'll continue to use throughout our lives.

Focus on values. The details of a person's life are interesting, but legacy coaches want values to surface. Facts give us information, but if we can detect values, we can form a connection that could become part of the person's legacy.

Recognize that formulating legacy is an intense, active process. Both for us and senior adults, figuring out legacy is challenging. We need to stay alert and help our seniors focus.

Note a person's developmental uneasiness. This concept alludes to the unconscious nature of the developmental tasks and the prospect of sorting a lifetime of experiences, which can feel daunting or overwhelming. If the elderly person is having difficulty with these tasks, we need to come to his or her aid.

Conduct these conversations in a variety of settings. If the elder person's health permits, varying the venue is extremely important to stimulate different memories to surface. Encourage as much interaction as possible.

Prevent the degradation of a person's experiences into a default legacy. Legacy coaches must intervene on behalf of seniors to hold control issues at bay. Battles for control can smother the ability and desire to get to legacy. We don't manage the legacy; we manage the process by which legacy is discovered.

Feel the emotional gravity of our seniors' attempts to review their lives. If we can imagine how seriously seniors take this look back, then we start to understand how important it is that life review in old age moves forward.

Tune into an elderly person's radar. Our elders can read us very well as having empathy and insight into aging, or not. They begin with the knowledge that we're not old people, so how do we know anything about their concerns? When we can convince them, through our legacy-coach approach, that we understand this process, we can feel their relief. Most seniors, once we assure them they have all the control they need and we're listening with our hearts, can relax and let their emotions flow.

Raise any subject that seems relevant. When talking with senior adults we know well, there are hardly any questions that would seem off limits or too personal to this age group. Declining health opens up the heart in ways we can't imagine. Most of the skills needed to facilitate life review involve the ability not to question and prod, but simply to listen and ask the right follow-up questions.

*　*　*

IN many of the anecdotes I've shared in earlier chapters, much was revealed that was unexpected but ultimately important to the older person's life review. Yet, most of the time I facilitated the discussion by remaining silent and simply letting that person talk. There are times I could have jumped into the discussion, but chose not to for a variety of reasons, including the following:

- The conversation took a nonlinear turn, signaling that something important was about to be revealed.

- Details emerged that presented a picture more vivid than a painting or a movie, indicating that this topic was key to organic legacy and worthy of intense focus.

- A subject was *not* mentioned that logically should have been, signaling that the person was still processing its meaning.

- A subject was introduced or dismissed with more emotion than it deserved, hinting that its importance but not its significance was understood.

- A matter was repeatedly mentioned, pointing to values the person wanted us to remember and help incorporate into the legacy quilt.

Much of the time, our elders need our attentive and sympathetic ear, not great conversational skills. Listening for the values involves just that: lots of sympathetic listening.

Discovering Our Own Life's Influence

We are rarely certain about how much influence we have on other people. Part of our legacy-coach mission is to open up life review so that we are able to discover how our elders influenced others. In doing so, we sometimes discover our own values—and begin our own life review.

A woman who taught high school in our town saw the obituary of a twenty-year-old man she recently had as a student. Even though Ellen didn't know the family well, she felt the need to attend the funeral and offer whatever words of comfort she could to the family. After the service the student's grieving father asked who she was. Somewhat hesitantly, she replied, "I didn't know your son well, but I taught him sign language in his last semester senior year. I wanted to be here today to . . ." To her utter surprise, her student's father smiled and hugged her, then said, "I'm so glad to meet you. For the last six months of Jeff's life, he couldn't talk, so the only way we were able to connect with him was by signing."

When my friend, Tom, was eight years old, a grocer defended him against a bully, something Tom's macho father wouldn't do, and he remembers that grocer as a hero to this day. The grocer has no idea the influence he had on this man's life, but the now-grown-up boy clearly remembers him as a model of manhood he tries to emulate.

These stories illustrate that we don't know the influence we have over another person's life, and one way to find out is to ask ourselves some of the same questions we're asking our elders and open ourselves up to all possibilities. This teacher will be remembered by this family as long as they remember their son, which is forever. This grocer is remembered by my friend every day, because he recognizes the importance of small acts of kindness toward a child and undoubtedly lives his life open to opportunities to repeat such acts. He himself will want to be remembered in this way.

"Discovering" and "creating" are powerful words for this legacy process. They are the drivers that uncover legacy, not, for example, of the grocer, but of the rescued boy, now a man, because the incident provides clues to what he values.

By helping our elders discover their values, we sometimes discover our own.

T. S. Eliot, at the end of *The Four Quartets*, comments on this process of life review when he notes that "the end of all our exploring" takes us back to the place from which we started and we view it as if for the first time. Arriving where we started and knowing the terrain for the first time is what happens when we search for legacy. We go around and around and around the events in our lives and come back to them and see them in a different way. In searching for legacy, we review those relationships and events—through the stories we tell and the memories we hold dear—that have given our life meaning. If we want our lives to be remembered, those values have to be understood and then passed on to the people who will survive us.

Organic legacy transforms lives, because the information contained in a legacy reinforces choices we've made, or guides us onto different paths. Such changes may impact others' lives for decades or generations to come. Knowing our elders is to learn about ourselves; facilitating them teaches our children about their destiny, as well as their duty, and the privilege that awaits them when we begin our own life review in a search for the legacy we will want to pass on to them.

Essential Q&A

Q: I know my dad misses my mom, his weekend golf outings with his buddies, and the freedom he had when he could still drive, but he never talks about it. In fact, all he seems to do is sit around and mope. What can I say to him that will spark his interest in life again?

A: Facilitate an unstructured conversation with your dad. Ask open-ended questions that give him the opportunity to bring up issues that matter to him, such as the losses he's recently endured. From his answers, try to discern what needs to become part of his legacy and help him find the connections that will fill the void he's feeling.

Q: What's the difference between the organic and political or default legacy?

A: The political and default legacies, discussed in chapter 3, are not necessarily heartfelt. There is little or no emotional connection the person has with the act. The default legacy in particular is a passive process. Because it is built posthumously, the deceased never has any input into it. I call it half a footprint and half a footprint isn't worthy of the lives our loved ones led. The political legacy is one the person is expected to form, and so "does the right thing." Such a legacy may be heartfelt and transform many lives, but does not necessarily do so.

We focused on organic legacy in this chapter because it is an active process that speaks from one heart to another and engages both the older generation and ours. It has the potential to transform many lives.

Q: I understand why I need to listen for the values, but I'm not clear about how to interpret what I hear. Any pointers?

A: Think of the different ways you would answer a factual question on a questionnaire or an open-ended question posed by someone you trust: To a fact-finding question you might give a two- or three-word answer. To an open-ended question you might never finish to your satisfaction. That difference in response illuminates our values. When talking with our elders, we have to listen carefully with our legacy-coach ears to what is repeated, what is emphasized, which details surface again and again, and how these details shift. If we think about their answer to a fact-finding question and compare it with their answer to the same question asked in a slightly different and open-ended way, we begin to see what they value. Those values can be used in forming their legacies.

Q: I've tried these open-ended questions, but they don't seem to work with my grandmother. Whenever I bring up a subject that I'm most curious about, she shoos me away like she would a pesky fly. How can I break through and get the information I want?

A: First, make sure all her control issues are resolved. Is there something about which she feels a sense of loss and hasn't expressed? If so, she may be focused on loss and regaining her balance and not have energy left over to probe more deeply into her past. Ask her directly what she needs. Next, consider that you might not be asking her the right open-ended questions. She may not be interested in talking about her father, but a question about her boyfriend at age eighteen might evoke memories that lead you to subjects you want her to explore.

Q: This legacy-coaching stuff seems time-consuming and laborious. Is it really worth the effort? What's the real value to the older person—and to us?

A: In medicine the dictum is: Cure when possible; comfort always. We can't *cure* aging, but we can offer comfort. We can't make old people better, faster, or quicker, but we can try to assist them *on a developmental level*. In doing so, we help them stitch together the legacy quilt they are compelled to create. It's their gift to us, one that we can later embellish and hand down to our children. How can we question the value of this legacy-coaching process that offers such huge emotional rewards?

APPENDIX I

A Note to Professionals

---

*"May I never get too busy in my own affairs
that I fail to respond to the needs of others
with kindness and compassion."*

—*Thomas Jefferson*

Early in my career, I worked as a physician's assistant in a busy family practice clinic in the West. One morning a woman in her mid-sixties came into my office, sat down, and looked at me with more apprehension than I usually saw in my patients. Her intensity told me to drop my clinical diagnostic approach. Instead, I relaxed, focused directly on her, and asked, "What's going on?"

She looked me in the eye and replied, "I've got a sore throat, and I'm divorcing my husband."

This section is directed to professionals whose practice involves dealing with the elderly, where communication challenges are formidable, yet crucial to understand and master if we are to succeed in our missions. It assumes we are familiar with the issues of control and legacy that drive our older clients' developmental agendas, and how those agendas may clash with our own. Certain communication strategies can be used to get to the core of the problem and make the time we spend with this age group optimally productive by enhancing opportunities for life-review facilitation.

It's important to let older clients set the communication pace. If we do so, then how do we manage this collaboration so that our time with them is productive? How can we implement the information in this book to meet our obligations to elderly clients and their families, as well as our own firms or practices? Before we can answer these questions, we need to take note of the special communication challenges professionals face.

Special Communication Challenges for the Professional

Time constraints: Doctors and nurses have endless piles of medical journals they rarely read. Lawyers, CPAs, and financial advisors suffer the same information overload. In addition to trying to stay current in their fields, professionals must address licensing and compliance issues that grow more complicated every year. There seems to be less and less time to do what we do best: take care of clients or patients. And now we are realizing, having read the previous chapters of this book, that in order to serve our elderly clients well, we must engage in nonlinear discussions that don't fit neatly into the time slot we've allotted in our agendas! A tall order, but a vital one if we are to serve this population well.

No previous knowledge of client's background or history with client: Very often, unlike a family member, we have no previous history or personal knowledge of this client, only what's presented to us on a summary sheet or in a bulky file. Here is where we need to use legacy-coaching skills to connect with the older person's core concerns.

History with client but presented with changing needs: Even when we know elderly clients well, they can present different needs that compel us to rethink all our previous solutions. It's important to understand the reasons for these changes so that solutions going forward will address and build upon life-review issues from which requests for modifications arise.

Paradoxes, enigmas, and laundry lists: Older clients may surprise us by the depth and complexity of their life review. Our first reaction might be to withdraw from what seems an overwhelming set of problems. However, our legacy-coaching skills help us appreciate that these lists may be an early phase of recontextualization and that we need to pay attention and help clarify the issues that arise. Not everything in a person's life develops in sequential order.

We need to listen for patterns that emerge from the innumerable details. The patterns contain the values senior adults want to pass on to future generations.

Family interference: Occasionally the client's family becomes an obstacle to providing sound advice. For instance, the family disagrees with the elderly person on whether to follow through with a prescribed medical procedure. Or the family disagrees with their planners' advice about how to dispose of certain assets. These situations can put professionals into uncomfortable situations, but if we are communicating well and our relationship with the client is solid, we can navigate these murky waters.

Inappropriate setting: Doctors' offices are sterile; they have to be. But the glaring lights and antiseptic smell can inhibit discussion of an embarrassing, perhaps life-threatening symptom. Lawyers' offices can be intimidating. Sometimes the problem with the venue can be as simple as too many people in the conference room to allow the kind of intimate dialogue needed to uncover a client's heartfelt wishes. Sometimes a change in venue is required to get the conversation flowing.

Clients' unfamiliarity with professional jargon: Basic concepts that professionals will understand can present big hurdles for clients and patients. Using unfamiliar terms is a sure way to prevent the connection we seek with clients. While we don't want to talk down to them, we want to use language that connects. Once we connect, we can communicate. Once we communicate, we can form the relationship that is at the heart of our mission to provide the services they seek.

When they uncouple, we've missed the mark: Particularly when their health status is murky, or the family isn't the entire legacy, the "straightforward" solutions we come up with will not ring true. Instead of the go-ahead, we'll get polite stalling or delaying tactics as answers to our proposals, which means we've wasted everyone's time. We need to revise our approach to get discussions back on track.

Rethinking Our Approach

It may appear that the communication techniques I offer in previous chapters of this book cannot work within the daily demands of the professional's world. Listening to all that detail, trying to discern patterns when the phone is ringing away, encouraging nonlinear discussions when it's hard to remember basic facts, are techniques that take time and the kind of mental effort we find difficult to summon during our busy days. But unless we tune in to what I refer to as the elderly person's developmental dialect, we cannot begin to appreciate the reality of their lives, or the fact that control issues and legacy opportunities are present in almost every conversation. The good news is this: All we need to do is *integrate one or two new communication techniques per visit* and we begin to see dramatic results. If we don't develop an ear for legacy opportunities, if we are unwilling to rethink our concept of aging and put into practice a modified communication style, we run the risk of providing incomplete and ineffective service. Ignoring the developmental mandates of older adults leads to predictable disappointments, frustration, and in some cases, disasters on both a professional and personal level. We ignore these communication tools and risk *increasing* the amount of time we need to spend with seniors to achieve our goals. Working harder with the same old skills we've been using is a waste of effort, because if the elderly are the dominate population for the next fifty years (and they are), then we have no choice but to learn how to effectively connect with them. But how do we do this with limited time, incomplete history, and the perpetual second-guessing of our efforts by well-meaning family members? What is a realistic plan?

Communication Rules for Professionals

Mind the (age) gap. While we are offering our expertise, they are looking at us as youngsters who cannot possibly understand the complexity of their lives. Offer language that addresses that concern:

   Example: "I've often been told I look youthful, but I assure you that I've seen and resolved many cases similar to yours over the past couple of decades and I would like to put my expertise at your command."

   Don't exaggerate our role. We are part of the fabric of an elderly person's life—an important part—but one of many individuals vying for the person's time and energy. The developmental mission of older adults is a process that unfolds in layers of time and through many relationships. No single professional is charged with the entire project.

Example: Consider how children progress through their developmental odyssey; there are a variety of players involved in every stage. Parents usually top the list, but other family members, friends, neighbors, teachers, and coaches all play a role. The key here is awareness. The more players who are aware of the developmental needs of children, the easier and more satisfying their journey to maturity is for everyone. The same is true for older adults. So we might address this fact of life this way: "I would like to make a suggestion, Mrs. Jones, and I want you not only to think about it, but discuss it with the appropriate people on your team."

Keep the horse before the cart. Sometimes our professional approach is ready, shoot, aim. That is, we offer them "simple," "straightforward" solutions, remedies, and options *before* we've heard their concerns, which embody the content of their unique developmental dialect and provide clues to the values they cherish. Their present situations are extremely complicated, filled with conflicts, emotions, and indecision about major life goals that we have no knowledge of, unless we ask. We must learn to understand and appreciate the facts before we act.

Example: We must gather clues to the content of their life review. To do so, we need to take a step back and ask open-ended questions to understand what's really going on behind the matters they present.

If they uncouple, we need to review our approach to help them uncover the truth of their lives. When the family isn't the entire legacy, the "straightforward" solutions we come up with will not ring true, and we'll get polite stalling or delaying tactics as answers to our questions, which means we've missed the mark and wasted everyone's time.

Example: "I see I've not produced an answer that you're satisfied with. If we were to try a different approach, where should we start?"

Get staff on board. Legacy coaching is *not* up to one person. Although at times an intimate, one-on-one conversation is necessary to move life review forward, the follow-up is a team effort that must involve your staff, other professionals, and the client's family.

Example: Confer with staff on the direction of your most recent talk with the elderly client. Ask for their feedback and use it.

Use legacy-coaching skills to promote life review. It bears repeating: Life review is not optional. The sooner we tap into the substance of a client's or patient's process, the sooner we develop the relationship that will yield the results we're seeking. There are several ways to promote discussion of life review. One way is illustrated in the following example.

The Secret Conflict

I recently consulted with an elderly man I'll call Ed who is quite wealthy. Ed's financial advisors were having trouble coming up with a plan that suited him to dispose of his wealth and they asked me to interview him. He regarded me with curiosity and asked me what my role was with this particular firm.

"I'm the guy who tries to figure out how long you're going to live, and I'm also the guy who tries to figure out what the rest of your life is going to be about."

"What does *that* mean?"

"Well, I am the legacy coach. Someone who reaches seventy-two, as you have, is being pressured by much younger people to make what look like fairly straightforward decisions. Yet I know for a fact that the present position you're in is extraordinarily complicated and filled with a lot of conflicting emotion and probably some major problems that have not been looked at for a long time."

A smile developed slowly across Ed's face and he said, "That's where I am."

I sensed I'd struck a chord, so I continued, "You've amassed millions of dollars by moving forward and now you're required to do a retrospective. You must now *weigh* your life instead of simply *live* your life, and it may not be a process you're comfortable with. Generally when people weigh their lives they see some things that humble them, but also may shame them. You are also being asked to make decisions about how you want to live out the rest of your life and how you want to be remembered. You've been described to me as 'hesitant' about going forward with the financial-planning process. When I see this kind of hesitation, it is usually caused by some major conflict in the person's life."

His voice changed, and he said, "I have a major conflict. I'm not comfortable discussing it, but it dominates everything that I do." He then ended the conversation, but asked me if I could meet with him privately at some point in the future.

* * *

WHAT'S interesting about this exchange is that when Ed asked me questions about the legacy process, he connected with my answer and was visibly relieved that the conflict he felt was a normal part of life review. The information that there was a legacy inside him begging to get out was as useful to him as anything else I could have said. In a different setting, with fewer people in the room, I will be able to sit down with him and ask the kinds of open-ended questions that could lead him to reveal and possibly resolve his conflict. My approach will reassure him that *his conflict is unique, but not new,* and possibly involves the fact that his family, for whatever reason, is not to be his entire legacy. He needs to work though his guilt about that and be prompted to think about some heartfelt alternatives.

The Two Rs

Ed's case illustrates that the two *Rs*—relationship and results—go hand in hand. No one at the financial institution took the time to develop the kind of relationship with him that tried to identify the source of his conflict, so it remained poorly described and blocked his ability to commit to any plan his advisors developed. The fact that he brought up his conflict is significant; to me it meant he wanted to discuss and resolve it. This initial conversation was a prelude to his search for organic legacy, a multistep process not usually accomplished in a couple of conversations or meetings.

It's important to remember that when an older patient or a client has this kind of hesitation about a professional recommendation, the person is asking to be facilitated in the search for an answer different from the ones we may have offered.

Ed's story is not just interesting; it illustrates the power of legacy coaching to reap rewards. Even a discussion of the dynamic itself can open doors.

Communication Tools for the Professional

Know the older client's emotional terrain. I've referred to several books throughout these pages. Become familiar with the contents of at least one, and preferably all of them:

- *Another Country: Navigating the Emotional Terrain of Our Elders,* by Mary Pipher, Ph.D.

- *The Greatest Generation,* by Tom Brokaw

- *Let Evening Come,* by Mary Morrison

- *From Age-ing to Sage-ing,* by Rabbi Zalman Schachter-Shalomi

These four books give us a rich portrait of the emotional journey the elder generation has taken, as well as a look at the values they embody.

Be patient. Allow seniors all the time they need to mine the depths of legacy. What looks like efficiency now by adhering to our scheduled appointments can come back to haunt us in terms of incomplete or irrelevant plans that clients may reject out of hand, sending us back to the drawing board. Allow specifics to emerge in the natural flow of conversation.

Keep a notebook to record details that emerge. Ask staff to do the same. Record in this notebook both the new ideas that seem relevant and details that emerge from conversations with clients. Sometimes amid all the verbiage we hear, it's difficult to find patterns of relevant experience. Yet in these patterns lie the values that the person is grappling with. It's important to feed these details back to elderly clients whenever possible and assess what kind of reaction we get—more discussion? An emotional outburst? A change of verbal direction? We need to gauge our subsequent professional advice based on their responses.

Offer control whenever possible. Do so by using the active verbs that offer control. (See chapter 9 for the list.) I found the *overuse* of these verbs yields even better results. It won't sound phony or repetitious to senior adults unless they sense we're being insincere.

Ask the right questions. The crafting of questions is of paramount importance to the professional in dealing with any client, particularly elderly ones. When we know a client over a period of time, we can pick up on changes in attitudes through the different nuances of questions they ask. (*"What was that plan you mentioned to me last year?" "Do you still think setting up a Roth IRA for my granddaughter is beneficial?"*) If the client is new to us, we must work hard on timing issues as well as on verbal and nonverbal cues to measure whether the person is receptive. Are we opening doors or shutting the person down with too much information?

How to Say It: A Professional's Guide

Here are some core statements and questions that offer control and the chance for legacy to emerge in discussions with senior adults.

- **"Tell me about yourself."** This statement is one of the most effective questions we can ask a client or patient as long as we pause and wait for the answer.

- **"What is the one thing I can do for you today that would be helpful?"** This question announces that we can focus on the primary issue, try to solve the problem, and get to other issues as time permits. It also indicates that the client has our undivided attention.

- **"What is the most important thing I need to know about you?"** This question announces that we are ready to wrap our professional service around the older person and not waste any time with ideas and solutions that would never work.

- **"Who is the one person, beside yourself, who knows you best?"** This question gives us both a significant person in the older client's life and another resource to tap to clarify information.

- **"Do you need more time to think about it?"** Even if we are up against time pressures, such as those a financial advisor might have in drawing up a new tax plan, we get better results by reminding clients that the opportunity is available, but leaving the decision to act under their control.

■   **"What would you do if you could do something about it?"** I'd do such and such, is the typical response. We might respond kindly, **"Well, why haven't you?"** Rather than seem rude, the question might provoke exactly the answers we're looking for. We need to listen to the reasons that emerge. These reasons offer clues to conflicts that may be key to unraveling a particular portion of the person's legacy.

When we hit a roadblock (and we will!), try a different approach. Reframe the problem in different language, much the way a litigator does when he realizes he's about to lead a witness or the judge sustains an objection from the opposing attorney.

Maintain a flexible schedule. The following anecdote, drawn from my practice, reinforces this communication rule for professionals as no other example can.

A Good Problem to Have

Mr. Smith is the head of a university foundation located on the West Coast. The university is near a large population of older adults who have come to the area for good weather and the low cost of living. Mr. Smith soon discovered that the normal hour-length appointment for his older potential donors was inadequate. Instead of trying to compress his meetings so he could squeeze more into a day, he adjusted to the needs of these clients and allocated more time for each interview. In fact, he blocked out two hours for each meeting and always arrived early, usually to find the elderly potential donor waiting for him.

Do not roll your eyes in exasperation—Two hours! Get real!—until you read below about Mr. Smith's results.

Mr. Smith has become an acknowledged expert at communicating with older adults. His success on one level is profound and humbling. By letting the elder donor set the communication pace, he has enriched and been enriched by his relationships with members of this age group. Using the communication tools and strategies outlined in this book, he has provided innovative reinforcements for the elderly person's battle for control. At the same time he has provided creative and effective facilitation in the area of legacy development. All well and good from a communication perspective, but what about his success as a fund-raiser? How is the university doing in terms of donations? It turns out Mr. Smith has created an unanticipated problem—that of too much success. Undoubtedly this is the kind of problem every businessperson would like to have.

The donations have been exceptional. The problem is that many of the older adults want to give *all* of their wealth to the university, but Mr. Smith must decline these offers for fear of reprisal from the donors' families. Why does he continue to have such success? Because he has connected with these donors' primary developmental needs. He has allocated the time, understood their developmental mandates, and fine-tuned his ability to focus and listen. With their children far away, the indifferent medical care they sometimes receive, and the artificial environment of a senior community, they find in Mr. Smith a person who brings compassion and effectiveness to their lives. He also brings impeccable ethical standards. Although flattered by the desire to give everything to the university, Mr. Smith helps these older adults discover other avenues for their legacy. He embodies the spirit and implements the skills of a legacy coach.

I have shared this story with groups of financial professionals who previously scoffed at the idea of such long appointments. Unbeknownst to me, one of them experimented with longer appointments for a few select clients. She reported that the expanded meeting times and her new legacy-coach communications strategies produced startling outcomes. Her business thrived. But she discovered that the most rewarding part of her efforts were her newfound friendships with older adults. She said these new perspectives changed her and, to use her own words, for the better.

We should all have these problems, correct? Time is crucial to us, but remember, that perspective changes when we get older. It is a fact we cannot ignore.

The Woman in Pain

How might we respond to the woman at the beginning of this chapter who, in the same breath, told me she had a sore throat and was divorcing her husband?

This is what she was communicating to me: "Treating me for either strep or a virus doesn't begin to touch the source of my pain. I'm challenging you to find out more."

My follow-up? "Tell me about it."

A lesson I learned early in my professional life was that, as in medicine, we cure or solve the problem when we can, but we must comfort the person always. Yes, our livelihoods depend on seeing as many patients or clients as possible, implementing plans, getting results. But we won't succeed at any of these missions with elderly clients unless we know how to listen to them in a way that responds to and enhances their end-of-life tasks. Employing simple but effective communication strategies is an opportunity for professionals to achieve spectacular results—both professionally and personally. This rewriting of the cultural definition of aging—listening for senior adults' developmental dialect and responding appropriately—helps diminish the isolation they feel. Legacy coaching can be used without restructuring a practice. All it requires is commitment toward certain goals to understand and communicate more effectively with older adults. With our goals and a commitment in mind, we can more effectively serve the needs of older adults.

Essential Q&A for Professionals

Q: It's all well and good to say that we need to "turn communication roadblocks into professional opportunities," but there are times when my open-ended questions don't seem to work. Am I doing something wrong?

A: There are several factors that can block legacy discussions with clients, including our lack of awareness of the issues in their life review. Do they have a major conflict that makes discussion uncomfortable? A conflict about the appropriateness of the discussion itself might trigger feelings of disloyalty to the family and block the flow. Assure the client that families are hit-or-miss, and may not be the way the person wants to be remembered. Sometimes we lack a sense of intimacy with elderly clients. Make sure control issues are not in the way by using verbs that hand control back to the client.

An inappropriate setting for the discussion, involving a room with bad lighting or with too many people in it, can inhibit discussion. Change the venue.

Q: *I have a client who has admitted to me that he has a major conflict regarding the disposition of his estate, but he won't tell me what it is. What should I do?*

A: Unblocking legacy discussions is a multistep process, and may need to be approached from different directions. Even if a client won't discuss the conflict, reassure him he's made a major step forward by admitting he has one. Assure him that the family is very often not the whole deal.

Be confident that if a client mentions having a major conflict, he or she *does* want to talk about it. Otherwise that subject would not come up. In order to facilitate that discussion, create a "safer" environment for this kind of legacy discussion to emerge. Start by changing the venue and the number of other professionals involved in this aspect of the discussions. Sometimes a one-on-one discussion on the client's turf will open up communication channels.

Assure the elderly person that in the right conversation, the issue will be resolved and the steps to take will be clarified. As mentioned earlier, approaching the conflict from a different direction can sometimes prompt a breakthrough. If not, instead of asking the person directly about it, ask about the vision he has of the result of dealing with it. What would the solution look or feel like?

Most important, assure the person his conflict is *unique, but not new.* The person who has this kind of conflict may have distorted some of the pieces. As legacy coach, our aim is to return a sense of proportion or balance to the puzzle.

A good technique, if appropriate to the situation, is to be prepared to share our own stories and values with elderly clients. Doing so creates the kind of intimacy that allows them to open up and reveal their own truths.

A last resort, and only if necessary, is to enlist family members or others who know the person well to give you some history that might shed light on the situation.

Q: I'm a medical professional and I often see situations where the family wants a more aggressive treatment protocol than the elderly patient himself does. I also run into situations where the family wants to discuss their elder's medical situation without their relative present, a violation of doctor-patient confidentiality. While I would never put an elderly patient through a grueling treatment without the person's consent, I find myself agreeing with the family at times about the effectiveness of new treatments. How do I communicate to my reluctant elderly patients that there are times when intervention may be wise?

A: Sometimes a "no" from an elderly patient is the warm-up answer, signaling the person needs some time to process the fact that he has yet another serious or life-threatening illness. Have your staff make follow-up calls or arrange for the elderly patient to come in for a two-week checkup to assess the situation and see if the person shows up for the appointment and asks questions, signaling he's done some thinking about his original decision. Using language that places control squarely with the patient ("Of course, it's *your* decision, Mr. Jones, whether you want to maintain control over this condition."), bring up treatment options again and see if there's been a change of mind. If so, proceed with control language in full display; if not, accept the patient's decision. As for family interference, if you think they can be helpful, include them, without revealing confidential information. Otherwise fall back on confidentiality of your relationship with the patient.

Q: How do I clue my boss in to the fact that scheduling one-hour appointments with elderly clients may be time-wise, but pound-foolish?

A: Results speak volumes. In this case, you may need to take on some of the thorniest cases in your firm's file and show that you can move things along by scheduling appointments your way.

An A-to-Z Reference of Terms as They Are Used in This Book

accelerating the agenda A noticeable increase in the intensity of the life-review process when health declines or there is some other change in a senior adult's circumstances.

age-based agenda The two conflicting psychological drivers of behavior, the resolution of which propels a person through each stage of the maturation process.

answer, warm-up The first answer, but not necessarily a well-considered or final answer, a senior might give in any time-sensitive or pressured situation, particularly concerning health and other major life changes. Warm-up answers do not invite immediate further conversation, but may be recontextualized and changed when the senior feels in control of the decision-making process.

baby boomers The bulge in the population born after World War II, now entrenched in middle age. Sometimes referred to as the "sandwich generation" because of the conflicting demands produced by care of aging parents and those of growing children and grandchildren.

communal society A social structure, no longer predominant in American culture, in which all generations of the extended family live in close proximity their entire lives. (From Mary Pipher's *Another Country*.)

communication A skill that uses verbal language and subtle nonverbal body movements to transfer information and convey emotions from one person to another.

communication radar A form of intuition most people possess in which they are able to pick up nonverbal information through body language, silence, and the way questions are posed. Seniors use communication radar to judge how receptive a listener is to their control and legacy concerns.

control A primary human desire at all stages of life that becomes an all-consuming driver of behavior in senior adults as they cope with profound losses on a daily basis.

control, loss of The waning of strength, health, peer-group members, and consultative authority as a person ages, compelling that person to fight to retain whatever does remain under the person's command.

crisis As used in these pages, the clash and subsequent resolution of conflicting tasks that propel an individual through a particular developmental stage. A subconscious driver of behavior, according to Erik Erikson. (See Notes for sources.)

departure rituals The timing as well as verbal and nonverbal activities that individuals display as they attempt to end a conversation; also known as "winding down." (See SETTLING RITUALS.)

details, attention to One of the five unique communication habits of senior adults in which they relate stories in vivid detail or repeat a story and embellish it with different facts. Attention to details is one way senior adults process moments of significance in their LIFE REVIEW.

developmental dialect The communication approach that recognizes differences in age-based agendas and attempts to connect two people; also known as learning to speak the other person's "language."

developmental orphans What senior adults become when forced to live in assisted-living facilities that offer little contact with caring adults and no understanding or facilitation of their DEVELOPMENTAL TASKS. The idea is based on Harry Harlow's work with infant monkeys who, when deprived of their mothers or any human cuddling or contact, fail to develop appropriate coping skills.

developmental tasks A usable, practical psychological profile of certain age-related actions and motivations that humans share at each stage of life.

developmental uneasiness The degree of resistance or reluctance senior adults have to the overwhelming demands of the life-review process, for fear of stirring up unpleasant or uncomfortable events or memories, or being unable to determine their significance. As long as they remain vigorous and healthy, seniors may retain some developmental uneasiness, but once health is compromised, they tend to focus and start life review in earnest.

elders See SENIOR ADULT.

end-of-life tasks Senior adults' developmental drivers—maintaining control and searching for a legacy—that must be addressed and resolved.

enhanced perspective The ability of senior adults to weigh and measure decisions informed by an entire lifetime of experience.

geriatric gap Lack of information in the popular culture about the profoundly important DEVELOPMENTAL TASKS facing senior adults; a cultural bias that assumes (falsely) that at the end of life, all faculties are in decline, and thus there can be no growth in the emotional and intellectual lives of senior adults.

health, loss of The signal that a senior adult is moving from the "young-old" to the "old-old" stage of life (according to Mary Pipher in *Another Country*), a time when the search for legacy accelerates. At this stage the heart opens up, life review takes on new urgency, and topics previously dismissed or forbidden become foremost in seniors' conversations.

identity crisis A popular term for an individual's difficulty in resolving the conflicting items driving a particular developmental stage.

jargon Verbal obfuscation, usually by a professional, that wrests control of a conversation from a senior adult and can result in UNCOUPLING. A legacy coach's role is to demand clarification of the jargon by the professional.

legacy The values by which we want our lives to be remembered. Searching for legacy is the primary psychological event of aging. The process emerges only when control issues are resolved.

legacy checkup A skill that demands legacy coaches ask the profound, open-ended questions needed to evaluate how far along in the life-review process a senior adult has progressed.

legacy coach A person with a set of specific communication skills that facilitate senior adults in their search for the ways they wish to be remembered, their primary end-of-life task.

legacy, default A legacy of natural consequences, revealed after death, in which the deceased person has no input or takes no part in shaping. Default legacies also form when the senior adult is consumed by control issues and never gets the chance to address legacy.

legacy ears The ability to ask questions of senior adults and listen closely to answers to discern the patterns and ideas that represent values by which they want to be remembered.

legacy, organic The heartfelt legacy, based on extensive LIFE REVIEW, by which the senior adult or deceased is remembered for the values he or she most cherishes and wishes to pass along to future generations; the unique footprint we leave behind by which we wish to be remembered. Organic legacy reconsiders things, events, and relationships that may have been misinterpreted, misunderstood, or unrepaired in a person's life, and sets those factors right. The goal—to be part of the conversation a century from now—usually must be facilitated by a LEGACY COACH.

legacy, political A legacy, usually more mechanical than heartfelt, formed by those who have completed a truncated form of LIFE REVIEW; also known as "doing the right thing."

legacy quilt Moments of emotional material, recollected during the life-review process and examined for content, quality, and values, that together make up the ways in which a senior adult wants to be remembered.

legacy vehicle An event, a decision, or a reconsideration of profound questions—even family stories—that need to be passed along to younger generations in a family.

life review The elaborate process in which elders engage to find something of value that they wish to pass along to younger generations, and by which they wish to be remembered. It is the dominant psychological event of old age, whether expressed (sometimes through unique communication habits) or unexpressed.

myth of diminished capacity A set of beliefs about old age that incorrectly assumes it is nothing but a long process of decline in intellect and mental function, that as the body goes, so goes the mind. Researchers have shown that the changes in mental capacity in senior adults actually enhance the life-review process. (See chapter 4.)

nonanswer A response that indicates no real meeting of the minds or resolution of a problem. Nonanswers are a hint that the senior does not have enough information to make a good decision.

nonlinear conversation One of five unique communication habits of older adults, in which they will pause, then deliver one or more complete non sequiturs. Although sometimes referred to as "off-topic verbosity," the pause and non sequiturs are a signal to legacy coaches that a value-laden statement is about to be expressed. Researchers have shown that off-topic statements move the content of a person's conversation toward issues of high moral significance.

patterns, searching for The process by which legacy coaches hear and determine from conversations with senior adults the values they cherish and by which they may want to be remembered.

pauses Silent beats or gaps in the flow of conversation. When senior adults pause in a conversation, very often they are forming a nonlinear thought about a recontextualized event that, once expressed, may need to become a part of their organic legacy.

plant-and-wait technique A communication skill in which the legacy coach notes a senior adult's resistance to an idea and backs off from demanding immediate compliance, an answer, or resolution of the situation, thus giving the senior time to process the request and find out how it fits into the LIFE REVIEW. Bringing up related subjects might prompt further discussion of the situation, but its resolution must remain under the control of the senior adult.

question, open-ended A legacy-coaching skill that can jump-start life review, recontextualization, and other powerful communication channels. The questions are "open-ended" because the answers rely on interpretation, memory, and values, not on facts. "How are you different from your mother?" is an open-ended question.

question, parallel circumstances A communication technique in which the listener is seeing connection with the senior adult, or wants the senior to consider options previously rejected. The intent is to learn from a senior's enhanced perspective, or to approach sensitive subjects from a different angle and encourage the senior to drop defensiveness about the difficult subject.

question, perspective A communication technique in which the listener offers personal information in the form of a question to the senior adult with the intent to appeal to the senior's wealth of experience, or to urge the senior to talk about a subject he or she may be reluctant to discuss.

question, ramping-on A follow-up technique to points heard in a conversation, used to extract more information or show sincere interest in the content. Ramping-on questions are effective in conversations with older adults in reinforcing their efforts to recontextualize events in their lives.

question, retrospective A legacy-coaching skill that allows the senior adult to engage in some form of RECONTEXTUALIZATION and LIFE REVIEW by stimulating nonlinear answers. "What would you have done had you not met your spouse?" is a retrospective question.

recontextualization the process in LIFE REVIEW by which senior adults look backward to prepare for their future, remembering long-ago events, people, places, and relationships, and assigning new meaning or importance of these events to their lives (from Zalman Schachter-Shalomi's *From Age-ing to Sage-ing*).

relationship, redemptive power of The notion that in helping seniors discover their most cherished memories and values, the legacy coach benefits, personally and professionally, by being able to incorporate and pass on these values to future generations.

repetition One of the five unique communication habits of the senior adult that signals an incident of great but not-yet-understood significance in the person's life. With each retelling of the incident, the senior adult relives the moment and clarifies its importance to his or her life review.

respectful detachment An attitude that legacy coaches adopt to allow senior adults to move at their own pace.

"secret stuff" The emotional and value-laden material, usually unexpressed, from a person's life that is needed for the organic, or heartfelt, legacy.

self-management The assumption that people can run their lives and thrive without any connections to other human beings.

senior adult The "politically correct" or currently preferable term to describe the seventy-plus-year-old parents of baby boomers, and the last to grow up in a COMMUNAL SOCIETY. Used interchangeably in this book with elders, the elderly, the older generation, etc.

setting The surroundings in which conversations take place. The setting of a conversation can enhance or inhibit substantive communication.

settling rituals The timing as well as verbal and nonverbal activities that individuals display before getting to the substance of any conversation; a communicator's equivalent of an athlete's warm-up that precedes a good workout.

spontaneous facilitation The ability of legacy coaches to rapidly shift gears, plans, attitude, and direction in response to senior adults' changing needs; techniques to employ when there is a spike in the older person's developmental agenda.

"terrible twos" A popular term for the stage in life in which toddlers express their difficulty in resolving the conflicting items on their developmental agendas—wanting Mom and also needing some independence from Mom—by throwing a tantrum or using other vociferous preverbal forms of communication.

tone The rhythm or inflection of speech, or the phrasing of questions, that supports or belies the meaning of the words that are spoken.

ultimatum A demand that seniors perceive as a challenge to their need for control and which rarely work in conversations with them.

uncoupling One of the five unique communication habits of older adults that signals a disconnect from, but not necessarily an end to a conversation. Although uncoupling feels to the legacy coach like rejection, it is actually a useful marker indicating that a new approach is needed. Using language that addresses seniors' developmental issues (maintaining control and searching for legacy) can restart the conversation.

urgency, exaggerated The attempt by those who interact with senior adults to "light a fire under them," that is, to force seniors to reach quick, rather than well-considered decisions; usually motivated by developmental drivers in midlife that command a person to accomplish a large number of tasks daily.

urgency, lack of One of the five unique communication habits of older adults that is frequently mistaken for indecisiveness, but is in fact a decision-making process that takes into account the complexity of the emotional landscape when a person reaches old age.

value-laden statement A recontextualized expression in a senior adult's nonlinear conversation that contains important clues to the life-review process and how the person wants to be remembered.

Notes

For readers who want to delve further into writings by and about senior adults, or who want more information about some of the ideas presented in these pages, the following references point the way.

Introduction

Mary Pipher's *Another Country: Exploring the Emotional Terrain of Our Elders* (Riverhead Books, 1999) is a source I frequently cite in this book; it is one of the most insightful and sensitively rendered looks at challenges aging seniors face.

Mary Morrison's *Let Evening Come: Reflections on Aging* (Doubleday, 1998) describes old age from a first-person perspective.

Chapter 1

For more information about the theories and crises of personality development, see the following sources:

Erik H. Erikson, *Identity and the Life Cycle* (W. W. Norton & Company, 1980). This volume is a collection of Erikson's writings focused on the crises of adult personality development. Another Norton volume of his writings, *The Life Cycle Completed* (1997), explores the ninth stage of development.

An introductory source for understanding Piaget's work is *A Piaget Primer: How a Child Thinks,* by Dorothy G. Singer and Tracy A. Revenson. A revised edition was published by Plume in 1996.

Chapter 2

Information about Résidence Yvon-Brunet is from "The Rights of Elderly People in a Nursing Home—A Little Creativity, a Lot of Respect, a Taste for Adventure, and an Allergy to Bureaucracy," by Germain Harvey, translated by James Lawler, in *Empowering Frail Elderly People: Opportunities and Impediments in Housing, Health, and Support Service Delivery,* edited by Leonard F. Heumann, Mary E. McCall, and Duncan P. Boldy (Praeger, 2001).

Chapter 3

This chapter's opening epitaph is from the poem "Night Mail," copyright 1938 by W. H. Auden, from *Collected Poems* by W. H. Auden. Used by permission of Random House, Inc.

For more information about recontextualization, see Zalman Schachter-Shalomi, *From Age-ing to Sage-ing* (Warner Books, 1997), pages 94–96.

Interview with Amy Dickinson was broadcast on NBC's *Today* on the day her column first appeared in the *Chicago Tribune,* July 20, 2003.

Chapter 4

More information about the aging brain is available in chapter 4 of Richard Restak's *The Secret Life of the Brain* (Dana Press and Joseph Henry Press, 2001). In that chapter, Dr. Restak reports on the research into the subject by Denise Park at the Center of Aging and Cognition at the University of Michigan, Ann Arbor, and Marilyn Albert of Harvard Medical School.

A recent source about Harry Harlow's work with infant monkeys is Deborah Blum's *Love at Goon Park: Harry Harlow and the Science of Affection* (Perseus, 2002). Blum won a Pulitzer Prize for an earlier work, *The Monkey Wars* (Oxford University Press, 1994).

See the citation in chapter 2's notes for information on Résidence Yvon-Brunet.

Chapter 5

For more information about the ways in which senior adults use nonlinear conversation, sometimes referred to as "off-topic verbosity," see Deborah Burke's research as reported in an article, "The Language of Aging," by Michael Balchunas, published in *Pomona College Magazine,* Summer 2000 issue. The article is also available at www.pomona.edu/Magazine/pcmsu00/16.shtml.

On the uses of repetition in conversation, see chapter 5, "Repetition," in James Hillman's *The Force of Character* (Ballantine Books, 2000).

Chapter 6

For more information about **functional ability,** see Chad Boult's contribution to *The Merck Manual of Geriatrics,* chapter 4 (John Wiley, 2000), quoted and found online at www.merck.com/pubs/mm_geriatrics/sec1/ch4.htm.

Good sources on the Internet for reliable medical information include the following: Centers for Disease Control and Prevention (www.cdc.gov), Johns Hopkins Medicine (www.hopkinsmedicine.org), Mayo Clinic (www.mayo.edu), and WebMD (www.webmd.com).

Chapter 7

I've referred to the movie *About Schmidt,* based on a novel of the same name by Louis Begley (Ballantine, 1997), earlier in these pages. The movie is worth viewing or reviewing in light of the discussion about the process of life review. After his wife dies, Schmidt begins a lengthy journey in which he revisits old places and relationships in an attempt to sort out what his life has meant. Thwarted in his attempt to connect with his grown daughter, he reaches out to a foster child in Tanzania, to whom he sends small monthly checks and writes voluminous value-laden letters, in an effort to find the meaning and connection he realizes his life has lacked.

Chapter 8

Information about the seven hundred thousand unique movements that the human body employs to produce nonverbal communication is cited in an article by Joanna Shalleck-Klein, titled "Nonverbal Body Language Does the Talking," published December 17, 1998, and available at http://silverchips-beta.mbhs.edu/oldsite/dec98/features/bodylanguage.html

Chapter 10

Author and NBC anchorman Tom Brokaw writes about the seventy-plus age group in his best-selling volume, *The Greatest Generation* (Random House, 1998). This is the generation whose dominant values—loyalty, patriotism, family, hard work—were shaped by growing up in the Great Depression, then surviving World War II.

Mary Pipher, in the previously referenced *Another Country,* discusses the loss of the communal society and its impact on the seventy-plus generation in chapter 3, "Time

Zones: From a Communal to an Individualistic Culture." For a discussion of the transition of what she terms the "young-old" to the "old-old," see chapter 1, also titled "Another Country."

T. S. Eliot's *The Four Quartets* is available in many sources, including *The Complete Poems and Plays, 1909 to 1950* (Harcourt, Brace & World, 1952).

Appendix I

The section Communication Tools for the Professional cites four references previously cited in these notes: Mary Pipher's *Another Country,* Tom Brokaw's *The Greatest Generation,* Zalman Schachter-Shalomi's *From Age-ing to Sage-ing,* and Mary C. Morrison's *Let Evening Come.* About Morrison's book: Its author, a professional writer with three books and six pamphlets to her credit, is an eighty-eight-year-old woman who writes about the aging process and its impact on the psyche from a vantage point most of us have yet to attain.

Index

About the Author

David Solie, M.S., P.A., is a managing director and medical director with Marsh & McLennan Companies. He is a licensed physician assistant with an advanced degree in clinical medicine. He was in private practice as a clinician in family medicine for four years before entering the life insurance industry in 1983 as a medical specialist representing impaired-risk clients. Since his transition from clinical to insurance medicine, he has dedicated the last twenty-seven years to extensive training in the areas of cardiology, oncology, neurology, and geriatrics.

Solie is a recognized expert in geriatric psychology, intergenerational communication, and extended life expectancy. His keynote and breakout presentations on communication between generations have won critical acclaim from audiences throughout the United States and Canada. His compelling stories, unique insights, humor, compassion, and inspirational delivery have made him a favorite of financial advisors, attorneys, accountants, health care professionals, senior service professionals, planned giving specialists, caregivers, and general audiences. His programs include:

- Unlocking the Communication Code of Aging Parents: Practical Communication Strategies for Working with Older Adults

- The Secret Mission of Baby Boomers: Practical Strategies for Working with Middle Age Adults

- When Are They Going to Grow Up?: Practical Communication Strategies for Working with Emerging Adults

- The Longevity Code: Eight Habits of People with Extended Life Expectancy

He is a graduate of the University of Washington, the University of Manitoba, and the University of Colorado Medical School.

ALSO AVAILABLE IN THE HOW TO SAY IT® SERIES...

HOW TO SAY IT® POCKET GUIDES

T17-0913